PROFILE OF A REAL ESTATE AGENT

by

Raymond W. E. Beaty

authorHOUSE®

AuthorHouse™
1663 Liberty Drive, Suite 200
Bloomington, IN 47403
www.authorhouse.com
Phone: 1-800-839-8640

First published by AuthorHouse 7/30/2007

ISBN: 978-1-4343-1330-0 (sc)

Printed in the United States of America
Bloomington, Indiana

This book is printed on acid-free paper.

PREFACE

Once upon a time, to protect herself from the big bad wolf, Little Red Riding Hood disguised herself as a wolf.

The wolf in order to sneak up on Little Red Riding Hood disguised itself as the grandmother.

And the grandmother, in order to confuse the wolf, disguised herself as Little Red Riding Hood.

The wolf, disguised as the grandmother, was able to get close enough to kill the grandmother, who was disguised as Little Red Riding Hood.

Realizing that Little Red Riding Hood was really the grandmother, the wolf was confused. The wolf disguised as the grandmother, then took off running through the woods.

Little Red Riding Hood, who was disguised as the wolf saw what happened and realized her grandmother was actually the wolf who began running through the woods.

Little Red Riding Hood, disguised as the wolf, took off after the wolf, who was disguised as the grandmother.

Hunters, seeing a wolf, who was really Little Red Riding Hood, chasing a grandmother, who was really the big bad wolf, shot and killed Little Red Riding Hood, because they thought she was the wolf.

The wolf, disguised as the grandmother, continued running through the woods.

Other wolves, thinking the big bad wolf was a grandmother lost in the woods, attacked and killed what they thought was a grandmother, but who was really a wolf.

When we don't know who we or others actually are, the results can be tragic!

This principle is not only true personally but professionally as well. Companies of all sizes lose market share, profitability and sometimes are forced to close because of their inability to recognize personalities that are involved. From their customers, to vendors, to in-house staff relationships, when there is no plan to identify what personalities are at work and what strengths and weakness are at play in those personalities someone is going to get eaten alive. Nowhere is this more true than in the real estate industry. The real estate industry is based on and survives on the professional's ability to recognize and meet the needs of the multiple personalities involved in a transaction. From the seller to the buyer, the finance person, other agents, title concerns, inspections, the list goes on and on. Only the real estate professional who understands their own personality and it strengths and weakness and also knows how to effectively and correctly identify the personalities of those involved in the transaction will be able to have a long and profitable career in real estate. What does the one agent who always seems to be in control have? The missing piece to the Real Estate Personality Puzzle. This book will provide you as a real estate professional the information you need to finally be in control of your career.

In the first book of its kind Raymond Beaty, a licensed Real Estate and Mortgage Broker and California's Premier Real Estate Trainer provides the definitive tool to real estate agents to give everyone access to the secrets previously only known to the top producers. Raymond Beaty has literally trained thousands of real estate agents. From providing exam preparation for the most difficult test in America to the continuing educational needs of professionals. Raymond Beaty's training facilities are recognized by the State of California Bureau for Private Post Secondary Education and the State of California Department of Real Estate. Raymond Beaty's real estate training experience provide the perfect opportunity for real estate professionals to finally have the science in their hand in a format that is practical to their industry to take all of the guess work out of the industry. How would you like to be absolutely positive that regardless of whether you were dealing with buyers, sellers or other agents you could ALWAYS be in control of the transaction? As you go through this book Raymond Beaty who is also a certified human behavior specialist will explain the science of human behavior and then with his real estate experience in the industry and in real estate training will teach you how to apply the science to your real estate career. In the pages that follow you will finally learn how to be in control of all the things you always wanted to have control of in a real estate transaction, who you work with, where you work, the kind of work you do, the kind of money you make, all come from learning how to identify your personality, its strengths and weakness. And how to correctly identify the personalities of all of those involved in the transaction. This is the tool you have been looking for.

CONTENTS

FINAL CHAPTER IS FOR BROKERS ONLY!

1

What Makes You Tick, What Ticks You Off
(The Science)

Human behavior science focuses on the emotions and behaviors of normal people. Basically, psychologist and psychiatrists try to help the 10% of people who exhibit self destructive behavior due to severe emotional trauma, a chemical imbalance, rebellion, or some other compelling reason in the person's life. Human behavior scientists explain the reasons and actions of the other 90% of people who do what they do because of natural and normal reasons. However, this doesn't mean normal people don't occasionally do abnormal things. Everyone is capable of abnormal behavior, but what most normal people do can be explained by understanding their personalities. Most of our problems would be avoided and or solved, if we simply recognized the truth of how our actions affect us and others.

On the other hand, abnormal people often do what they do because of deeper drives and compulsions. Those with abnormal behaviors are encouraged to see qualified professionals who can help them.

The science of why people do what they do focuses on the reasons we feel and respond the way we do. Just as the science of biology reveals the classifications of biological life – genera, species, phyla, and kingdoms – so the science of human behavior reveals that there are classifications of behaviors. There are also hundreds of different elements in chemistry. Each one is different, but they are all part of the Periodic Table. There are many different cloud formations in meteorology. All scientific classifications represent predictable responses to various situations, and in human behavior science, there are identifiable, predictable personality types.

The Myth and Mystery of Motivation

There is a myth about the science of motivation. The myth is: "we can motivate others." Coaches give stimulating pep talks to inspire the team to win the game. Teachers may try to persuade students to do better by scolding them. Parents may restrict their children's freedom, hoping to force them to improve their grades. These tactics may motivate some, but not most.

The truth is that we can't motivate anyone to do anything he doesn't want to do. People do what they do because of their own reasons, not ours. We can try to manipulate and intimidate (which are wrong), but we can't motivate them. Manipulation and intimidation often backfire. Using outside force to get people to do things can boomerang to hurt and haunt us. All true motivation is intrinsic, it comes from within. People are motivated by their own feelings and for their own reasons.

Have you ever said, "I wish my child was motivated!" or "If that person was only motivated to....!" Everyone is motivated, whether they take the particular action we want them to take or not. Some children are motivated to study; others are motivated not to study. The decision to act or not act is driven by the will of the individual. It is incorrect to say some people are not motivated because they did not take a particular action.

Motivation is not the ability to scream until people give in and do what we want. It is not a pep talk before a game. Motivation takes root and becomes personalized before we ever go into action. It begins with our personalities, that is, why we do what we do. The key is creating the climate and environment, which make people want to do what they should do.

People err in thinking that motivation is an art. You have perhaps heard of the so-called "art of motivation", but motivation is actually a science. Art is a free expression, which changes from medium to medium or person to person. Science, on the other hand, is observable and repeatable. Science doesn't change other than in predictable and controlled situations. The "art of motivation" is actually the "science of motivation" because most people have predictable patterns of behavior. Their behavior is obvious and calculable.

Art is also a rendering of reality, not reality itself. A person can paint another's person's feelings on canvas, portray them in drama, or express them in many other art forms. The form and expression change according to the medium, the crowd, and the performance, therefore it is more art than science. In science, you can predict the outcome and observe continuity.

The mystery is how to motivate others. Actually you can't motivate anyone because everyone is already motivated in his or her own way. Good motivators are those who do not intimidate or manipulate. Instead, they create the climate and environment that encourages people to perform at their personal best. That is what a good coach, teacher, parent, boss, preacher, or leader does to get people to respond.

Researchers tell us 85% of a child's personality is formed by age 6. By the time children reach the age of 21, their personalities are set. Only what we call S.E.E.s, Significant Emotional Experiences, change an individual's personality. If you were a happy go lucky 21 year old, you will probably be a happy go lucky 81 year old. If you were a crabby and complaining 21 year old....you probably won't live to be 81! There is much to be said about a child's personality, and the need to influence it when the child is very young. The challenge is to identify children's bents and lead them according to their personalities. The key is knowing how to read people and manage them according to their motivations, not ours.

There Are No Bad Personalities Just Different Personalities

Comprehending the dynamic differences will profoundly affect our lives. Our personalities are the unique ways we think, feel, and act: the way we are "wired" to respond. No personality is better than the others.

Someone is probably thinking: "But you haven't met my mother-in-law!" or "You don't know my boss!" Perhaps these people are terrors. However, it is not a rotten personality, but rather how they use their personalities, which makes them behave so poorly. I don't believe anyone has a bad personality. I believe we receive the essence of our personality from the beginning.

People are different. That may seem like an obvious, simplistic statement, but our grasp of this fact has dramatic consequences in our relationships. In the simplest delineation of the differences in people, we observe that some are motivated by accomplishing task and some are motivated by relationships. To illustrate this, let's say a task oriented person and a people oriented person are both working in a garden. Someone walks up and says, "Hi, how are you? What's happening?" The task person predictably responds: "I'm busy," or "Come back later." He is so concerned about getting the job done that he doesn't want to talk.

In contrast, the relationally motivated person might respond: "Good to see you! Time for a break. Let's talk"

She doesn't care near as much about getting the garden done as enjoying relationships.

Imagine a married couple planning their first vacation together. The wife is task oriented, but he is very relationally oriented. Before leaving on the trip her first question is, "Do you have a map?" He replies, "I don't need a map honey I have been there before." She says, "How far are we going to drive each day?" He sighs, "I don't know. Until we get tired." She says, "Where are we going to spend the night?" He moans, "There are hundreds of motels between here and there!" She says, "How much money will we need for food and lodging?" He explodes, "I don't know! And I don't even want to go anymore!"

She is task oriented and he is relationally oriented. She likes to plan and prepare, he likes risk and adventures. We can apply these two personality types to the work environment. Imagine a boss telling two workers (one task and the other people oriented) the project must be completed by 5:00 or they will be fired. Task oriented people refuse to be interrupted, and they work until the task is completed. But relationally oriented people have to control their natural drive to talk when they are interrupted.

Both are important to society. Can you imagine the world full of only one kind or the other? If there were only task oriented people, a lot would get accomplished but with little compassion for others. If there were only relationship-oriented people, little would get accomplished and even the satisfaction of the relationship could become frustrating without seeing anything accomplished.

While technology is advancing, relationships are falling apart. The computer has generated an accelerated growth in the sciences, the least of which is human behavior.

THE REAL ESTATE PERSONALITY PUZZLE

(Applying The Science)

As a format to help you understand the science that is being shared for the first time with real estate professionals, I will be using the concept of a listing appointment. As real estate professional we are all familiar with the process that goes into "getting the listing". You have heard many different formats and undoubtedly paid hundreds of dollars for different presentations so you would have the advantage over the next agent. Throughout this book I will be using the terms I have trained thousands of agents to use to understand the listing process, then we will couple the process with the newly discovered science and you will be years ahead of any other professional in the industry. The three words I will use over and over in each section are, SEEKING, SELLING, and SIGNING. These three words encapsulate the entire real estate industry whether you are working with buyers, sellers, other agents, title companies, your broker or any of the many relationships necessary to complete a transaction.

SEEKING

Science makes it perfectly clear from a scientific standpoint in the previous section that holding out for some way to motivate anyone to do anything against what they are already motivated to do is a complete waste of your time. Although that is what the majority of agents spend their time doing. Let's begin with the seeking process. Your business success depends on your ability to find the next client. There are literally hundreds of programs and materials that have flooded the market designed to help you find the client you are seeking. What if you knew exactly where to look, who to look for and how to get the client to respond to you? Understanding the mystery of motivation is the key. Buyers, sellers, other agents, everyone is motivated by what motivates them. Mass mailing, cold calling, in general doing things that you have been told would work or that might have actually worked for you does not answer the question of what motivates others. YOU HAVE TO ANSWER THE QUESTION THEY ARE ASKING. The only way to do that is to understand the four basic categories that people fit into in relationship to what they need.

As a broker for many years I have seen agents work their sphere of influence, network outside that sphere with contacts from the first sphere and on and on it goes, all the while seeking that one person with that one approach that will land them the next deal. Exhausting, isn't it? When I started training my agents to identify personality types, understand what that personality type needs, and deliver that need or answer that question, the client list increased by 35% immediately.

In the next chapters as I explain from my background in behavioral science what these four personalities are, I will show you how to revolutionize your business in a matter of months so that you are no longer seeking the unreachable with a disconnected message.

SELLING

The critical practice of understanding what really motivates people is made the most obvious in the process of selling. How many times have you been on the other end of a phone conversation where someone was trying to sell you something you neither wanted or needed? From car lots to appliance stores, to clothing, sales people have been trained in this guerrilla warfare style of selling that no one really wants, but we endure it to get the product or service we need. YOU CANNOT SELL PROPERTIES THAT WAY! I know you have seen the aggressive real estate agent that moves a lot of properties because they won't take no for an answer. Check their status 3 years later to see if they are still in business. Statistics support that they are not for one reason or another. Reason one, they develop no residual business because when the transaction is over people realize they have been bullied and they don't want that experience again. Reason two, they are exhausted from chasing new business because they have no old business. Reason three, when the smoke clears on the transaction studies reveal as many as a third of their transactions are sent to arbitration which becomes expensive, exhausting and time consuming. You can push clients down to get what you want, but remember the real estate reverse law of gravity, what goes down, WILL come back up! Either in your brokers office, the local board, the Department of

Real Estate, or as more and more agents are discovering, the hallowed halls of justice!

I have had dozens of agents say to me over the years, "I don't understand why your clients still like you after the transaction is closed, by the time I am finished with a deal everybody wants my head!"

Here is a novel concept, try selling the client what they want. The reason selling in the real estate industry has developed such a negative connotation is because real estate professionals do not know how to identify what people want and why they want it. Solve that mystery of motivation and the client and the sale are yours!

SIGNING

Signing is a broad term I use for – closing the deal. Closing the deal encompasses a number of different relationships. It is not just about getting the name on the contract, it is about the environment you create around you. From your client, to the other agent, their client, any one involved in this transaction needs to feel and believe that everything is going to have a happy ending. The signature from anyone at any stage of the transaction represents for the person signing that everything is going to be alright. The problem is as real estate professionals often times we use that same old approach to force all parties involved to agree to what we want or believe is best in the transaction. Then throw up our hands in disbelief and frustration when we find ourselves running around trying to put the deal back together again! That happens for one reason, NO ONE IS REALLY SIGNING! You worked really hard to get signatures but no agreement.

Agreement only comes when you have provided all the necessary parties with what THEY need and want. Until you can become proficient at identifying what people want and need you will always be re-signing.

I see hundreds of agents every month in my training sessions. When I tell them this dynamic they say things like, "the client said they wanted such and such a house at this price and I found it for them." Or the client said, "they wanted this price for their house and I got them that price." Or the other agent said, "if I could do this or that then the deal would work." If it were that easy then anyone who could mark things off a to-do list could be a real estate professional. You must be able to identify the personality behind the request, what motivates that personality and what satisfies that personality before you can have agreement.

How would you like to know for sure that the escrow is closed even before the official close date? How many other transactions could you generate if you were not dancing around the last transaction making sure nothing goes wrong? Signing means closing the deal, closing the deal means getting agreement, getting agreement means knowing what that personality is and what it wants and delivering.

Raymond W. E. Beaty

2

An Ancient Discovery For Modern Times
(The Science)

The terms personality and temperament are synonymous. When we use these terms, we are referring to patterns of thoughts, feelings, and behaviors. There are many theories about personality types. After much study, I chose to use the DISC Model because it is simple to understand, easy to remember, and practical to apply.

Understanding our active or passive roles helps us identify our specific temperament styles. By combining these two different categories of influences (active/passive and task/people), we end up with four specific types.

Everyone has a predictable pattern of behavior because of his or her specific personality. There are four basic personality types. These types, also known as temperaments, blend together to determine your unique personality. To help you understand why you often feel, think, and act the way you do, the following graphic summarizes the Four Temperament Model of Human Behavior.

Some people are easily identifiable as extroverts or passive introverts, but many of us are confused because not all extroverts are active toward people. Some are active in tasks. In the same way, introverts can be passive in relation to people or tasks. Understanding the four quadrant model of basic human behavior sheds light on this. It can make the difference between the right and wrong response and a proper or improper behavior in any given situation.

Hippocrates, the father of modern medicine, first observed four unique temperament types, or specific patterns of behavior. He thought it something to do with the chemical makeup of the blood. To describe the four types, he used Greek words which have been Anglicized as: Choleric, Sanguine, Phlegmatic, and melancholy. Many others who observe human behavior have categorized people into four temperaments, but personality types have nothing to do with the color of body fluids. Temperaments are a mixture of nature and nurture. You can correlate the Greek terms to the DISC model:

D is the Choleric

I is the Sanguine

S is the Phlegmatic

C is the Melancholy

Our personalities should never become an excuse for poor behavior. The attitude of many is, That's just the way I am. Love me or leave me. You knew I was like that when you married me, but we shouldn't blame our rotten reactions on our personalities.

Each temperament style represents a specific behavior pattern. How we use or abuse or personalities determines our effectiveness with others. Once we understand the four-quadrant model of behavior styles, we can begin to identify our individual profile. To simplify the four types of temperaments, we will use William's DISC titles. The following are the four quadrants of the DISC model:

D - active/task-oriented

I - active/people-oriented

S - passive/people oriented

C - passive/task oriented

Disc Descriptions

Here is a simple description of each of the four types of behavior represented by the letters D-I-S-C. A strong or high type behavior is more obvious and predictable than a weak or low type.

D Behavior

D behavior demonstrates itself in determined leaders. They can take control of a situation, make quick decisions, and cause things to happen. If they overuse their strengths, they can become dictatorial, demanding, or domineering.

I Behavior

I behavior demonstrates itself in optimistic people who lead by inspiring, influencing, and inducing others to follow. They may be characterized by overconfidence, talkativeness, and a craving for popularity. These individuals tend to comprise their beliefs due to peer pressure.

S Behavior

S behavior demonstrates itself people who are stable, submissive and steady. They don't like change and are extremely loyal. The most tolerant of all, these people are often timid and too agreeable.

C Behavior

C behavior demonstrates itself in people who are cautious, calculating and conservative. They are seldom wrong because they are slow to decide. However, these individuals tend to overanalyze and be too critical of others.

Strengths and Weaknesses

Keep in mind that 85% of people tend to be composites of DISC, therefore, most people will be blends and combinations of the characteristics evident in the four personalities. There are numerous variations of this model. Speakers, writers and trainers have added their own titles to make the model more simple or personal, but this four vector explanation of basic human behavior has become universally recognized. The DISC personality profile was originally designed by Dr. John Geier and has been validated by the Kaplan Report and Winchester Report. The DISC profile and Model of Human Behavior stand out as the most reliable and practical available today.

Basic Overview of the DISC Model

High D

Basic Motivation:
Challenge

Environment Needs:
Freedom
Authority
Varied activities
Difficult assignments
Opportunity for advancement

Responds Best to a Leader Who:
Provides direct answers
Sticks to business

Stresses goals

Provides pressure

Allows freedom for personal accomplishments

Needs to Learn That:

People are important

Relaxation is not a crime

Some controls are needed

Everyone has a boss

Verbalizing conclusions helps others understand them better

High I

Basic Motivation:

Recognition

Environment Needs:

Prestige

Friendly relationships

Opportunities influence people

Opportunities to inspire people

Chance to verbalize ideas

Responds Best to a Leader Who:

Is a democratic manager and a friend

Provides social involvement outside of work

Provides recognition of abilities

Offers incentives for risk taking

Needs to Learn That:

Time must be managed

There is such a thing as too much optimism

Details are important

Humility is a virtue

High S

Basic Motivation:

Security

Environment Needs:

An area of specialization

Identification with a group

Established work pattern

Stability of situation

Consistent, familiar environment

Responds Best to a Leader Who:

Is relaxed and amiable

Allows time to adjust to change in plans

Serves as a friend

Allows people to work at their own pace
Answers "how" questions
Clearly defines goals and means of reaching them
Gives personal support

Needs to Learn That:
Change provides opportunity
Friendship isn't everything
Discipline is good

High C

Basic Motivation:
Quality

Environment Needs:
Clearly defined task
Sufficient time and resources to complete task
Explanations
Team participation
Limited risk
Assignments that require precision and planning

Responds Best to a Leader Who:
Provides reassurance
Maintains a supportive attitude

Provides open door policy

Defines concise, detailed operating standards

Needs to Learn That:

Total support is not always necessary

Thorough explanation is not always possible

Deadlines must be met

People respond to discovering their personality types in many different ways. Some people find it fascinating; others find it frustrating. For some, identifying their temperament is easy. For others, it can be extremely difficult. Some people are more obviously one or two personality types, but others are a complex blend. If your personality fits into one or two categories, it is easier to identify and understand your specific personality. Most people quickly recognize their strengths and uniqueness, but some feel they are a little of every type. This may cause confusion. Evaluation is not always easy, so be honest with yourself and focus on those characteristics which are obvious. Descriptions which don't fit. Narrow it down to one or two types which best describe you.

Your personality even shapes your response to this study. "D"s are sometimes proud of their type. "I"s tend to be more excited and talkative about their personality. "S"s are more shy and quiet. "C"'s are usually the most doubtful and confused.

Some people are afraid to identify their personalities. I try to reassure them that their assessment is not a test and there are no wrong answers. They can't fail it. It simply profiles his or her personality types, and no one has a bad personality. A few people have had bad experiences with psychological testing, and they feel hesitant to try another tool. Basic temperament assessment, however, is not a clinical measurement. It is designed for people who simply want to understand a little more about themselves and others.

KIM, HOLLY, JOSH AND SAYAR

To illustrate the importance of understanding others, picture a teacher asking his or her class the simple question, "Who discovered America?" There are all different types of personalities in the class.

Kim, the high D yells out, Columbus. Next question! The teacher responds, "Why did you yell out like that, Kim? Why don't you raise your hand like everyone else?

Kim likes to take charge. She wants to be in control. She wants to get everything done in a hurry so she can go play.

The teacher ask again, "Who discovered America/" Holly the high I jumps up, waving her hand, and says, "I know, I know. Call on me, teacher! Please!"

She responds, "Okay Holly, who discovered America?"

She acts like she knows, but says, "Oh, I forgot. It's right on the tip of my tongue. Can you give me the first letter?"

She wants to turn it into a game like Wheel of Fortune.

The teacher sighs, "Oh Holly, put your hand down and stop acting like a clown.. Why do you always raise your hand without having anything to say?"

Holly responds with a surprised silly face and sits down while the class laughs at her antics.

The teacher then ask Josh, the high S, "Who do you thing discovered America?"

Softly Josh says, "I think it is Columbus, but I am not sure. If anyone else knows and wants to say, it is okay with me. And if you don't like Columbus, I am sorry. I hope this doesn't make anyone mad."

Finally, the teacher asks Sayar, the high C. "Do you know who discovered America?"

Sayar gives the teacher one of those disgusting glares and blurts out, "Now what do you mean by that question?"

Every child responded according to his or her personality. Each one had a predictable pattern of behavior. This is an age-old truth with modern applications.

THE REAL ESTATE PERSONALITY PUZZLE

(Applying the Science)

It should go without saying at this point that you need to stop and take the Real Estate Personality Profile provided with this book. Understanding your personality type will be the first step in being able to identify other personalities and your way to manage your personality for the most productive result.

SEEKING

Once you understand your personality the seeking process becomes extremely easy. Remember seeking is not just looking for the next client; it is that process where you are looking to build a business environment that attracts clients, (because you know what they need). You attract the right partners, (because you know what they need). You attract the most profitable business, (because instead of pushing, you are attracting, BECAUSE YOU KNOW WHAT THEY NEED)! In the next chapters we will deal with one personality type at a time so you understand how to use your personality and the other parties as well. In this chapter let me give a brief overview of how understanding the personality types will affect your business.

In the seeking process if you understand that a D client is going to push you at every opportunity to exercise their will in the transaction you have a couple of options. You can push back because after all you are the expert in this transaction, or you find ways to put the D client in a position that their need to lead is met and you still keep the money. That is the point of a transaction isn't it? Or perhaps you are dealing with a D agent on the other end of the deal. Classic showdown at the real estate corral. You have a fiduciary responsibility to your client, you have your own personal pride and you have this tyrant on the other end of the process sabotaging your deal. If you shoot it out you can put another notch on your belt, (your gun belt that is because your money belt will be empty) or you can find ways to give the D agent ceremonial leadership and still ensure the transaction stays alive. We are not talking about manipulating. Just orchestrating. Have you ever wondered why a professional orchestra needs a conductor? Think about it, these are professional musicians, the best in the world. Do you really think they need someone to help them keep time? Or someone to help them count their notes, or when they are too loud? Musicians play all of the time without conductors, why is it so necessary at the symphony level? Because they are all experts with their own personality and needs. Someone has to make sure they all work together in concert with what they have. If you will pay attention to the process I am showing real estate agents for the first time, you will be making sweet music all the way to the bank.

SELLING

Being aware of your personality type and being able to identify the personality of the party you are dealing with will determine if you sell or fail. Let's suppose for a minute that you are a strong D. It is okay; remember there are no bad personalities. You are a strong D and you are making a listing presentation to a strong C. You make your presentation based on your strong leadership style, promising to always be available, take control, deal with all of the problems so the seller will not have to be concerned. Great for you because you get to be who you are naturally. Not so great for the client because that is not what they are looking for. The strong C wants to know all of the details. You say don't worry I will handle of the details; the client says how will you handle all of the details? You say years of experience have taught me to be in control of the transaction so you don't have to worry. Client says I never worry because I always know what is going on, so tell me, what are the details.

You as an agent are completely frustrated because you are offering this incredible service and the client just isn't getting it. The client gets it, you are the one missing the signals, (and also not getting the listing), because you failed to realize that your D, while helpful and familiar to you, does nothing for the C who wants you simply to tell them what you are going to be doing and keep them informed along the way. Just because this approached worked very well on your last client, who by the way was a strong S and wanted someone to take control, does not mean it will work every time. Just a few well placed questions early in a conversation will allow you, if you are paying attention, to immediately identify personality types of the clients, the agents, the escrow coordinator, the office manager, the title officer, the broker. Any party that is a part of the closing of this transaction can be given the information they need, in a format that is important to them, if you are learning the lessons of this book.

SIGNING

So everyone is at your office sitting around the conference table and you are about to hear the offer from the other agent. You are a D; the other agent is a D. Your client the seller is an S, the buyer, who is in the room as well is a C. There are a least a dozen different ways this deal could go sideways. You and the other agent could start positioning yourself for control of the room. In which case you are overlooking the major issue of your fiduciary responsibility to your clients. The battle could rage for 30 or 40 minutes before you even address the topic of the offer. Rest assured, and I know you have seen it before, if you do not recognize what is going on, the deal is out the window. The C buyer begins to ask about certain details that C's want to know about, you as a D see it as attempt to take more control so you refuse to give the information. Refuse to give information to a C and the deal is dead. Your S seller hears you start suggesting multiple options to resolve the conflict and it scares them to death because it sounds a little risky to them and this is the first time you have ever mentioned it. If you don't have the tools to identify personalities, it's over.

Let me give you a real life example of how knowing your personality and being able to identify everyone's in the room gives you the edge to sign, or close the deal.

I am a Licensed Real Estate and Mortgage Broker in the State of California. We deal with large numbers on the west coast and lots of laws. It is difficult enough given the money involved and the litigious nature of our state to close transactions without having deals blow up because of personalities. Including myself, there were four D's in the room. A top producing agent from an enormous firm, two old ranchers who were as tough and wild as the 6000-acre ranch we were negotiating over. It all came down to an old non-working D8 Caterpillar that was parked by one of the ponds. My D seller wanted an additional $2500.00 for the cat just because this guy wasn't going to give anything away to the other D, just because that is the way D's do business. The D agent and buyer were not about to pay $2500.00 for a tractor that didn't even work, because that is the way D's do business. This could have gone on for hours and probably been the death of the deal. But with my super powers of identifying personalities, (you will be a superhero when you finish reading the book), I announced that I had a solution. I announced that I had always wanted a Caterpillar and I knew someone who could repair it and I would pay the $2500.00 and come and pick it up tomorrow. D seller is happy because it cut into my commission, (that he never wanted to pay anyway), D buyer is happy because he doesn't have to give into D seller over a tractor, D agent is happy because he is going to get paid. So instead of a $50,000.00 commission I got really abused in the transaction and *only* receive $47,500.00. All for knowing what is going on in the room. P.S. Guess who came to see me after he bought the property and was ready to subdivide it into lots. I will teach you how to learn and harness your personality, learn and compliment others personalities, consider your commission check a graduation present from us.

3

Controlling The Dominant Personality
(The Science)

When you think of the people who seem to be natural leaders, who accept challenges, who are involved in many different projects, and who are more task-than people oriented, you are thinking of high "D"s.

'D"s are:
Dominant
Direct
Determined
Demanding
Doers

"D"s push for results. They shape the environment by overcoming opposition. They are very active, and they create aggressive environments, striving and pushing under pressure to get the job done. They constantly challenge the status quo. Their motto is, "If it doesn't work, change it." They take charge, they want to be in control. They were most likely the self-appointed captains of teams growing up.

"D"s want control and authority. They often believe they know how to do things better than anyone else and instinctively take charge, but they also work well under authority if they respect their superiors and remember who is the boss.

These determined people need challenge and prestige to fulfill their dreams. They seek opportunities for individual accomplishments and work their way to the top. They become CEOs, owners of their own businesses, or top managers in any field, club, or organization. Even if they don't climb the corporate ladder, "D"s end up telling everyone what to do. They can be found ordering others how to dig a ditch or organize a local union.

Dictatorial

"D"s tend to be dictatorial in their approach. They don't like anyone to step on them. They have the ability to dream, but they usually aren't strong in following through with the details. They would be more effective if they would develop skills of delegation. For "D"s, stumbling blocks are stepping-stones. Nothing is too difficult. They want freedom from controls and supervision, so they often become their own bosses. They move fast and hard and are the most prone to become workaholics. Confronted with conflicts, they are quick problem solvers, but they seldom calculate all the risks or consider all the options.

"D"s are instinctively impatient. They don't put off until tomorrow what they can do today. They push forward despite time limitations. Often misunderstood because of their active, task-oriented, optimistic personalities, these driven individuals are often tough skinned and hard nosed. Their emotions can be extremely intense.

"D"s sometimes seem to accomplish the impossible. They aren't quitters, these driven people love a challenge and are very competitive. They have a do or die attitude toward life. As active extroverts, they like to be where the action is, they are unable to sit still for long periods of time. Most of all, they love to direct the actions of others. As task oriented individuals, "D"s absorb themselves in projects rather than people. Often they seem to intimidate people in order to accomplish their task. They use people to build their work, rather than use their work to build people. It's not that they don't care about people. They are just more concerned about the project. People are a means to the end of getting the job done. Dominant types are impatient and easily irritated by those who are indecisive. They like strong leadership. They seem to relish debate and defiance. Tell "D"s they can't do something, and a startling metamorphosis begins to take place. They can turn into monsters! They will attack!

They need to be more calm and understanding of other's feelings. "D"s are often too straightforward and frank. They need to think before reacting. To improve their effectiveness in relationships, these people must control themselves rather than trying to control others.

Who's the Boss?

A high "D" will try to control someone with a low "D" score and make all of the decisions. The other often sheepishly obeys. Low "D"s willingly follow along in submission until their most serious concerns are challenged.

Low "D" people find it very difficult to confront high "D"s. Their preparation for battle is accurate information to prove their point. Presenting high "D"s with analysis usually causes them to look more closely at the conflict and be more rational. "D"s greatest influence over others is their ability to accomplish goals. Though careless at times, they usually still produce results. They tend to make people nervous because they are producers, pushers, and movers. They make great achievers if they don't self-destruct. They often speak before thinking, but surprisingly, they often come up with unique and immediate solutions. These results give them the confidence to fly by the seat of the pants. Other people, however, don't feel comfortable with this free wheeling style, so "D"s need to be more considerate others perspectives of the task at hand. Absorbed in task oriented projects, "D"s often create high casualty rates among subordinates and co-workers. Their pressured pushing to get everyone to move in the same direction is often demeaning to others who prefer to be treated as individuals.

"D"s are sometimes great motivators and challenging speakers, but their greatest concern is "reaching the mark, not touching the heart." By learning to balance their penchant for tasks with concern for people, "D"s can be much more effective leaders.

Though "D"s occasionally delegate work, they usually feel compelled to do everything themselves to maintain control and have it done "the right way." Once they learn to spread the responsibities around, they should supervise but not smother those who are contributing to the task. One of their biggest faults is taking back delegated responsibilities. To "save" a project, they may take back control and offend the one who was placed in charge. "D"s need to learn to communicate the purpose, plan, and process more effectively with others. Unfortunately, they believe the myth that everyone else thinks and feels as they do.

Slow Down and Explain

Once a decision is made on how a task should be accomplished, "D"s should tell others the reasons behind their decisions. Though they may be convinced and confident of that decision, others may not be. Clear and patient explanations enhance a person's role in leadership. It's not enough to say, "Because" or "I'm the boss." Reasons and specific plans need to be verbalized for everyone to feel secure in the decision. "D"s need to pace themselves and learn to relax. Vacations provide the needed balance for their high stress levels. Physical conditioning is vital because stress is one of their worst enemies. They are often unaware of the tremendous pressure they put on themselves to produce, and they are prime candidates for heart attacks and hypertension. Learning to relax and enjoy life should be a part of their plan to succeed.

Most importantly these driven people need to learn to prioritize. Working overtime and seldom pausing to appreciate their mates and children is hazardous to their health and wealth. The twin tyrannies of urgency and expedience are dilemmas they must avoid. As weekend mechanics with finely tuned machines, "D"s seem to race through life without the worries of blowouts. They are most effective when they slow down, calculate the risks, weigh the options, and receive wise counsel from others. Reflection and balance will protect them from their volatile emotions which can ignite their dynamite personalities.

"D"s need choices. Parents and teachers of high "D" children need to harness their energy. Relate to them with respect for their ability to decide for themselves. Give them the opportunity to be leaders. Don't stifle their drives. Point them in the right direction, give them parameters, and watch them fly. These driven people are the best doers anywhere. They conquer life's greatest challenges, but unfortunately they seldom conquer themselves. When you think of steel and velvet, dominant people are characterized by steel, but they need to be sensitive to others. "D"s are drivers plowing their through life, but they need to pave their way with pleasantness.

THE REAL ESTATE PERSONALITY PROFILE

(Applying the Science)

SEEKING

Don't worry too much about looking for the D client, they will find you. You can do a great deal to be attractive to the D client by the way you advertise your services. One of the fastest growing segments of the real estate industry is the "do it yourself" real estate company. Each year they capture more and more of the market share and most agents believe it is because clients are too cheap to pay their commissions. People have been paying real estate commissions forever. Studies show the majority of the people opting for these kinds of services have the money for the commission, what they also have is a personality that thrives on being in control. If you really wanted to recapture a market that is incredibly profitable you would simply allow these parties to be more involved in the transaction. Think about the properties you have seen attracted to these "do it yourself" services. It is not just the people who are a little too tight on the net sheet to make it work out, usually they are upper end homes with clients who either run their own business or are in upper level management. They consider it an insult to be told they need someone else to handle what appears to them to be a relatively straightforward transaction. Granted they may not know all of the ends and outs, but give them credit for their position in life and pay especially close attention to the D in their personality and give them some control.

This is also true when dealing with that D agent. I know you see them everyday. Remember, these people, like you, are running their own business. It takes a special kind of person to run his or her own business. You need to provide the other agent as much room as possible to give them choices. If you do not, a strong D agent will run right over you just for the pleasure of running over you. D's will sacrifice commission to win. I will say it again, and I know you have seen it before; D's will sacrifice commissions to win the personal battles. If you use the knowledge of identifying D's you can arrange the transaction in such a way that they look like they are winning but you are still getting paid.

SELLING

The most obvious way to sell to a D client is DON'T. D clients do not want to be sold, either on your services as the listing agent or your find for their new home. I know you really can't believe anyone would make the right choice without your services, but remember you responsibility is to the client not your sense of what is right for them. D clients will crawl over broken glass to get what they want; your best bet is to not be in their way but a part of the process. Another way to make this clear for you is to ask you to think about new developments. Ever wonder how large development companies get to be so large? They do personality research. Why do you think new developments (especially in gated communities) have these lotteries and limited releases for homes or home sites. They have done their market research; they know that the people who will be buying at this level live off the competitive juice that feeds a D. Tell a D there are only 12 sites being released. You can start counting the money. Use this information in your business to recapture a lucrative market that is slipping away from most agents.

Now I am going to tell you something that will save your life, increase your income and make all your days at work happy days. Are you ready? All brokers and owners of real estate companies are D's! There are some I's who try it but they are never in business for very long, (I will explain why in the next chapter). There are some C's who are calculating enough to run businesses but do not enjoy the constant physical contact of caring for agents and clients so they go back to being accountants. S's don't want anything to do with it so you are stuck with D's! Now how can I make your life better with this knowledge? Think about it, if you understand the science that I have explained about D's there are certain things you never want to do now that you know you broker or manager is a D. Refer back to the list of how D's react in certain situations. This means, are you ready for this, this means you actually get to control a D because you can predetermine how they are going to react! Your professional career would be greatly enhanced both personally and financially if you understood exactly what that person in the corner office needs, or how they are going to react, or better yet how you could get what you need. Have you ever seen a smile on a person's face that made you feel like that person knew something you didn't know? Smile.

SIGNING

Closing the deal with a D is a matter of letting them decide when the deal is done. This applies to every level of the relationships involved in the transaction. Let me show you what it looks like. You are making that great listing presentation of yours. It has a lot of information about how incredibly gifted and talented you and your company happen to be. Just when you are about to get to the part in the presentation that you enjoy the most, (it is the part where you have sold a gazillion dollars worth of property), the client interrupts and says, "how long will this take?" DDDDDDDDDDDD! That is the alarm that should be going off in your head. If you do not stop right then and there and begin asking the client certain questions we will be talking about later, the deal is over. After years of training new agents, nine times out of ten they will find a way to get back to their presentation. The client just gave you the most obvious clue you need to shut the presentation down, find out what they want to know, give them the information in such a way that they are in control of the decision making process.

Same process for the offer. Buyer says, "This is the one". You sit down and begin to instruct the client on what would be the most attractive offer. You are giving the pros and the cons, the possibilities and the strategies and just about the time you are about to get to the big finish the client says, "here is what I want to offer". There is the D alarm again. And again, after training thousands of new agents in classroom settings their immediate response is to try help the buyer understand why that may not be such a good idea. You know how easy it is for a client to get up and go find someone else who will write his or her offer. PAY ATTENTION! If you have a D buyer on your hands simply say, "I will write whatever you want I am *your* agent, here is what is probably going to happen if we submit *your* offer. And when it happens just the way you said it was going to happen and the offer gets rejected because you allowed the D to be in control, guess who magically allows you to be in control for the rest of the transaction. D's will always be in control, unless of course you recognize that they are a D and then .... well, you know.

4

Calming The Inspiring Personality (The Science)

Perhaps the easiest temperament to identify is the "I". You will find them leading, entertaining, and somehow adding to the positive atmosphere of every occasion.

"I"s are:
Inspiring
Influencing
Interested in people
Impressive
Inducing

Naturally uninhibited, "I"s love to express themselves. They are the clowns of the class and the life of the party. Often raised in a family atmosphere that encouraged them to share their talents openly, "I"s are performers and people pleasers. Their charisma and abilities to sway the crowd make them naturally persuasive speakers, salespersons, or actors.

"I"s who work in sales positions sometimes have difficulty closing deals because they don't want to be rejected. A "no" is a blow to their pride. Although "I"s give the impression of high ego strength like "D"s, they are much more sensitive to being hurt and manipulated than their domineering counterparts. Their charisma and ability to communicate only gives the illusion of inner strength.

"I"s are the people who make small talk in the checkout lines at supermarkets. While other shoppers look for the shortest or fastest lane, "I"s enjoy the opportunity to socialize with people. They like to help other shoppers in the store whether they work there or not. If someone looks confused, "I"s naturally respond, "Can I help you?" They enjoy making people feel good.

Cheerleaders at Heart

"I"s are cheerleaders. Even when they are not up front, they stimulate those around them. They are natural spark plugs. They generate tremendous enthusiasm, and they entertain people. "I"s want to help others to feel good or accomplish a goal. They love to participate in a group where they can stand out. "I"s often take control of a group, not because of a strong desire to have their say, but because others won't. In order to avoid feeling uncomfortable, they naturally step out and lead.

These influencers prefer environments which include acceptance and social recognition. They are very friendly and enjoy backslapping, hugging, and encouraging others. They fill the air with laughter and joy. Recognition is a strong incentive for "I"s. They desire the freedom of individual expression to win approval. They unique ability to speak spontaneously about anything and everything often gains them recognition in crowds. They can be found in an abundance of group activities outside their jobs. Where there is a crowd, there is an "I". Relaxing alone is not their style, they need and seek relationships. Because of their friendly demeanor, their interest are often crowd centered.

Work Environment

"I"s will never be slaves to time. They don't like time controls because they have trouble pulling themselves away from people. The task at hand is never as important as the people with whom they want to talk. Details are often seen as stumbling blocks. They are really concerned about new opportunities for recognition and acceptance, so opportunities to verbalize their proposals or ideas are very important to them.

Their strong need for favorable working conditions frustrates them when they are confronted with adversity. High "I"s need to concentrate on the task at hand. They are easily distracted, especially if they are working alone.

"I"s are often tempted to help someone or just stop and talk rather than work productively alone. They need others who respect their sincerity. They tend to give confusing messages about themselves, and they are often misunderstood as being proud or cocky. In reality, they are very sensitive to what people think.

"I"s need to focus on facts because many of their decisions are based on emotions. They need to learn to collect more information and consider all the options before coming to a conclusion. Being surrounded by others with systematic approaches to problem solving is very beneficial to these inspiring people. They need others who can deal with details and design the systems of follow through to accomplish task. "I"s make great ideas employees. They can be extremely creative, but they need to focus on getting the job done.

Strong Feelings

Because "I"s are primarily guided by feelings, they need to focus on the process of decision-making and individual follow through. They are easily distracted and tend to be undisciplined and disorganized. Training themselves to sit down and think on their own is an important step in their work habits. Instead of constantly seeking an ear to listen to them, they need to do more research in order to become more self-efficient.

"I"s need to practice taking a more logical approach(rather than the social approach) to their problem solving. They need to learn to demonstrate individual stick-to-it-ness. As promoters and persuaders, "I"s have the ability to spark interest and enthusiasm in others for just about anything. If, however, they lack the drive to see task through to completion, their energy and power of persuasion are wasted. They should constantly strive to perfect their follow through and complete what they have started. Organizational skills to help them manage their task include clock watching, scheduling, and personal planning.

Some "I" children are misunderstood by their parents. These excitable, enthusiastic kids may be tagged "hyperactive" but in reality, they are only being themselves. Parents of "I" children need to give a lot of positive strokes because these kids need more approval and recognition than others. Pessimistic parents can be very discouraging to these sensitive children. Interactive parents make great encouragers, but poor examples.

"I "s tend to be too dramatic, and as parents, they can be screamers. Their overly expressive behavior makes "I" children reactive. "I" parents need to learn to control their emotions and be calm. Children learn how to react by watching their parents, so screaming parents usually produce screaming kids.

"I"s need to control their time more wisely. They are often defeated by the clock, overwhelmed by the pressure of schedules and deadlines because they mismanage their time. They should realize that there isn't time for everyone and everything in the day. Thinking ahead and planning for interruptions are practical steps. Because they talk so much, they usually take a lot of time to complete a task, so they should give themselves more leeway. It is wise for them to set time limits and schedule earlier deadlines. Talking does not always solve problems or accomplish task. In fact, conversation often prolongs a project. In order to be productive, "I"s must learn the value of solitude and silence. Those who plan time alone can better manage their natural ability to interact with others. Also, they should respect the time restrictions of other people's schedules. Silence is an important commodity for these people to acquire. They will become more objective if they will think before expressing themselves. They should consider the amount of time and thought they have given a matter before coming to any conclusions. Although they tend to get away with things because they are popular, they should strive to be "slow to speak and quick to listen."

Competing Partners

"I" spouses tend to be too communicative, and they can be too sensitive about feelings. "I"s often want to know what their mates are thinking, but they seldom wait for answers. When a person tries to express themselves, they interrupt and never let him finish. "I"s need to be patient and focus on the other person. They also need to be careful not to concentrate on what they are going to say as soon as the person pauses to take a breath.

"I" partners compete for airwave, and they can also compete for attention. Two "I"s in a marriage or working relationship can become jealous of each other. They must learn to appreciate one another's talents and be willing to learn from each other rather than constantly tell each other what to do. They sincerely want to express themselves, but they need to remember that the other person may have the same desire. A little understanding and a lot of patience can go a long way.

Because "I"s are sensitive, they tend to avoid offending people. They need to learn that being firm and honest can be more important to others than being friendly. They have a keen sense of the mood of groups of people. This makes them natural leaders with the ability to inspire and influence people. Their friendliness is a blessing at every function.

Sources of Conflict

"I"s over-promise and under-deliver. Desiring to please everyone, they build high expectations, and people are often disappointed by their unfulfilled promises. When ask to do something it is better to respond, "I would rather let you know than let you down."

They also struggle when they don't get the attention or credit they deserve. If they feel overlooked, they can be very expressive about their disappointment.

THE REAL ESTATE PERSONALITY PUZZLE
(Applying the Science)

SEEKING

These are the easiest people to find. They are often described as the "life of the party". That means a lot to you as you determine how to work with an I as a client. The way to have this client base seek you out is to basically promise to put these peoples names up "in lights". There is nothing an I seller or buyer enjoys more than the actual recognition involved in the transaction process. In the mail outs and communications you provide to prospective clients, if you wanted to have an I client call you before they even finished reading your promo piece, promise to mention them personally in the advertising process. Promising to highlight the seller along with the property is the way to their heart and the bank. I's love it! There it is, in the weekend edition of the paper, the I with his family and dog sitting on the porch of their lovely home for sale. An I may not even realize he is actually selling his home, but he does know you have introduced him to everyone in your office, ask about his life and put his picture in the paper. He is in heaven.

The same is true as you seek out buyers to work with as well. "X Company is looking for a few selective buyers who will be featured in this weeks newspaper as highly qualified buyers". Every aspiring actor, class clown, life of the party, attention grabbing, center of the universe personality you can imagine will be scrambling for your attention. Now before you accuse me of taking advantage of people's weaknesses, remember as a licensed broker I am bound by law to provide a service to my clients that in the end puts the product they want in their hand. There is no more responsible way to do that than to know exactly who they are and the way they want that product delivered. When you are involved in the seeking process for I people, do yourself a favor, what I really mean is, do your client a favor and give them a trip down the red carpet for their fifteen minutes of fame.

SELLING

"Here is how that would make you look". That is the hypnotizing phrase to be used at every level of the transaction. I's want to know how that would make them look to others. I know that we have been dealing primarily with buyers and sellers, and I will continue to use them as a test case as we work through these principles. But you should begin to be able to make application to all of the relationships in the transaction. And I will devote an entire chapter to making sure you understand you and how to apply that to your business. But back to the two groups you spend most of your time and energy on. You are making that listing presentation to the prospective client. You notice they ask a lot of questions that include the word I in it. How do I, when do I, why do I, I,I,I,I,I,I,I,I,I, guess what? They are an I! So instead of you answering, "okay here is how *I* would handle that", you say, "okay here is how that would make *you* look".

The I buyer is looking for the same sort of confirmation and identification. Agents get really caught up in the

3 bedroom, 2 bath, great location, good school mantra. They think that is what everyone wants. And while that may fit the general description of the bulk of sales in America, it comes nowhere near describing WHY people want that. If you knew that the buyer you are dealing with was an I, you could sell them the traditional house, (you could sell them any house), if you could help them see how this house would make them look their best. Look the best in the eyes of their family, their community, and their colleagues. You say, there you go again using this poor persons desire to be seen, as a weapon against them. I say to you again, you are not their parents, you are their agent, if the most important thing in the world to this person is that they look great, help them look great. If real estate professionals could learn how to take themselves out of a transaction, put the I in the center, they would finally understand why there is no i in check.

SIGNING

It is no industry secret that the key to long-term success in the real estate industry is residual business. Clients who come back to you year after year and refer their friends and family to you. Now that you are beginning to understand the different personalities and the applications of those personalities to your business, here is your first big test question. Since referral business, for residual business is the key to long-term success, who do you think talks the most? Who do you thing likes to be heard because they love an audience? Which of your client's personality types will provide you the most unsolicited free advertising? It's me, me, no, it's **I**.

Closing the deal for an I client in such a way that they felt like they were the star of the show will provide years worth of referrals on the I talk show circuit.

The I seller will keep copies of the newspaper ads than ran with his picture in it to show all of his friends what you did for him, (he is really doing it to show that he is in the picture). The I will be forever grateful for their fifteen minutes of fame and will tell the story at every social function he attends. Church, work, the club they belong to, your ability to recognize their need and deliver based on their personality has provided them a lifetime opportunity for which they will gladly demonstrate their innate ability to take center stage and tell with skillful and mesmerizing passion the story of your service to them.

Your I buyer will be as equally grateful for a chance to have not only a real estate agent at their disposal but their own personal talent agent as well. Someone who has outlined their deal for them and the way it would make them look. Someone who has provided the necessary stage for the I client to successfully complete that latest performance. If you were looking for the most far reaching, impressive, long-term communication to the world about your services you only need to understand the history of communication, Telegraph, Telephone, Tell an I!

Raymond W. E. Beaty

5

Stimulating The Shy Personality
(The Science)

The highest percentage of people fall into the category
of the passive, people-oriented type of personality. They
are shy and reserved, but they often make the best friends
and most loyal employees.

Perhaps you have heard of individuals who took the
blame for things they did not do. They willingly accepted
punishment, even though they are not guilty. History
has given us many lessons of those who suffered for the
sins of others. Loyalty motivates some people to suffer
for the wrongs of others. They would rather endure
pain themselves than allow others to hurt. This can be a
wonderful quality, but it can also be a dangerous fault.

"S"s are:
Stable
Steady
Security-oriented

Sensitive

"S"s emphasize cooperating with others to carry out task. They are submissive servants who usually end up doing what the "D" has dreamed and "I" promoted. "S"s are soft hearted and sensitive. They may be seen as timid, but they are tireless in their labor. They let others lead, they avoid conflicts, and they strive for the status quo. Change is difficult for them, so innovation and creativity are left to others.

These people prefer sitting or staying in a single place. Their passiveness is often perceived as laziness by extroverts, but they are steady workhorses. They quietly get the job done while others push, talk, play, or criticize. "S"s don't like to make waves. Instead they work to calm them. Tranquility in the midst of turmoil is their specialty. Their staying power is incredible. While others lose their patience, nothing seems to unravel these steady, reliable people. They seldom openly show their feelings, and if they do, they cry quietly or laugh to themselves. Patience is more than a voluntary virtue; it is a way of life for them.

"S"s are extremely loyal, and they often work with the same company for years. They also tend to be family oriented and dedicated to their loved ones. Interest in their families is evident by the photos and mementos covering their walls or desk.

"S"s don't like aggression or antagonism. Their strong sense of loyalty however compels them to come to the aid of family or friends who are in trouble. They ardently defend them physically and verbally, stepping out of their comfort zone, shocking themselves and others.

They are not interested in showing off in a large group. They tend to seek out personal relationships, talking one-on-one or to a few people at a time. "S"s have the ability to listen for hours about anything. They are people-people with the ability to work while they talk or listen.

Calm in the Storm

Calming excited people and making others feel comfortable seems to come naturally to "S"s. They are not high strung, and they usually make great marriage partners and employees because of their concern for a steady and stable environment. They respond calmly to aggression, often defusing problems with their sincere interest and self-controlled temperament. They seek cooperation rather than control. As peacemakers, "S"s are servants who work patiently and persistently to resolve conflicts between people.

Because they have the patience to develop specialized skills, they often learn skills that others do not. "S"s appreciate routine rather than despise it. Their ability to do the same thing repeatedly makes them specialist. Concentrating on the task at hand is a great strength. They don't become easily bored because of their ability to concentrate on getting the job done.

"S"s want high touch not high tech. They want to support and serve, maintaining the status quo routine because they feel insecure with change. New things, especially high tech things, are threatening to them. They work best under controlled, stable environments. "S"s usually don't make a big deal about anything. They do their work well without fanfare. Sincere appreciation and consistency make them happy because they desire an environment, which includes security. Safety is imperative, and they shudder at the thought that someone could possibly get hurt.

One of the most important environments to preserve is the home environment. "S"s require minimal work infringement on their home life. They desire 9:00 to 5:00) work schedules, and they want their weekends to be free.

Status Quo

Detailed procedures are important to "S"s, and they prefer environments where they can consistently operate without confusion. Because of their need for security, they desire limited territory. Familiar, comfortable surroundings give them more confidence. Their sense of comfort comes from predictable patterns and familiar situations. They often withdraw from new challenges to avoid the risk of failure, and they are usually slow to speak and appear less active than others. Without standardization and simplicity, they may become unsettled and insecure.

"S"s need more organization than explanation. Once procedures are clarified, they can follow them better than extroverts. They even enjoy the simple tasks that often frustrate others, but everything must be explained and organized for them in a simple understandable manner.

They need exposure to people who react quickly to the unexpected. Because of their slow responses, they need to build relationships with those who can handle sudden challenges as well. By understanding their own apprehension about change, "S"s can adapt to a situation more easily. Reacting quickly is sometimes just as important as reacting smoothly, therefore they can benefit by observing those who respond more quickly to opportunities or difficulties.

"S" should stretch themselves to meet the challenges of an unexpected task. Their need for stability should not stifle opportunities to serve others. Though they are uncomfortable with change, they can respond to unexpected situations if they understand their natural reluctance. To stretch themselves, they should become involved in more than one thing at a time, not allowing their insecurities of a situation cause them to withdraw. They are capable of many tasks with the proper scheduling of time and space.

Supervising "S"s should include constant reinforcement. They usually prefer for others to take on new jobs and challenges, but they need to realize their own capabilities and have confidence to tackle new opportunities. They probably can do a lot more by exerting a little more confidence.

Lean On Me

Known as "Flip Phlegmatics," "S"s tend to flip back and forth according to the amount of pressure put on them. Their easygoing nature is so flexible that they may give the impression of having no convictions or strong emotions. Since they seldom respond outwardly to pressure, they provide a welcome balance to bold, outspoken people. They need to become more assertive in unpredictable circumstances.

"S"s need to be more assertive and less sensitive. Rather than avoid confrontation, they should learn to respond more assertively. They need to overcome their fear of being intimidated by others. Since many people are "S"s, situations often arise where there are all Indians and no chief. When a need arises, someone must take responsibility and assume leadership. Someone needs to become decisive rather than quietly waiting for other people to respond.

The "S"s greatest weakness is being naïve. They have trouble saying, "No!" Everyone knows that they will do what no one else wants to do because they care so much about pleasing others. I personally admire "S" behavior the most because it happens to be my greatest need. I respect their ability to stay calm. Unfortunately, their slow response and laissez faire attitude are often misunderstood as wishy washy, but their loyalty and calm are great strengths.

"S"s however, can be doormats for aggressive, insensitive people. If you are an "S" and live and work with someone who abuses you sexually, physically, emotionally or verbally, I strongly encourage you to get professional help. You must learn how to be strong for yourself. Do not try to just wish the problem away, it won't go away until you do something about it. Do not try to solve it overnight, you can't just put your foot down and demand that things change. Significant change takes time, planning and courage.

Assertiveness training courses can help. Recognize that your best attribute can potentially become your worst liability. Beware that your strength of being a servant does not become the weakness of subservience.

"S"s enjoy relationships with people who contribute to the task at hand. Though they are willing to do it all themselves, they work best as a part of a team. Getting input from others adds security to their environment. They are prone to become caught up in conversation and neglect their work, but they are willing to work all night to accomplish a job, especially if someone else will work with them.

"S"s need co-workers who are flexible in their work procedures. Bosses may demand the task be done their way, but these people often feel that they work better alone and without pressure. They are comfortable when doing the job at their own pace, and others would be wise to give them some flexibility. However, they need to learn to adapt to changing situations. Conditioning them to change increases their productivity. Sometimes the rules change halfway through the game, but that doesn't mean it is time to stop or slow down.

Relating to "S"s

"S"s respond best to warmth and friendliness. They don't like to be pushed into anything, so give them time to changes. They make wonderful Sunday school teachers, but don't change their room or curriculum half way through the quarter! They are slow to make friends because they initiate relationships. They listen well, but you have to ask them questions to get them to talk. Show genuine interest in their family and friends, be patient and kind. Try to see life as they do, and you will probably enjoy life more. Learn from them, relax, don't attack people, don't fight back, slow down and smell the roses.

Life is simpler to "S"s, but they are not simple people. They may be very talented, but you may never know it because they don't like to show off. Encourage them to share their talents in a small group before asking them to perform in front of a large crowd.

THE REAL ESTATE PERSONALITY PUZZLE

(Applying the Science)

SEEKING

The best way to find an S is to open your eyes. They are everywhere! Since they are not that hard to find the real seeking question turns out to be, how do I get them to seek me? It still never ceases to amaze me that agents really believe that people want to know who they are, not what they can do for clients. In an attempt to get clients to seek them out, agents put their names on bus benches, (not their services), post their pictures on grocery carts, (not their services), take out newspaper ads to tell everyone they love dogs, cat, apple pie, etc, (say nothing about their services). If by chance someone does call (because they were riding the bus on the way to the grocery store while reading a paper), when the agent shows up at the door clients always wonder, if **you** are the agent, who was that great looking person in the advertising? An S wants to know how safe am I going to be in this transaction? What services do you provide that will give me a safe, steady and secure transaction? Why do you care what an S wants? Because that is where the majority of your business is going to come from!

And if you wanted to determine out of this largest pool of clients if the majority of S's are male or female, guess the correct answer to these questions and you will be on your way to controlling the largest sub group in the largest group of people in your marketplace. You are showing the husband and wife the property, they are both looking interested. After the showing is over, you leave in your vehicle, they drive off in theirs and the first one to speak is? You are right, it is the husband. The first question he asks is? You are right, it is, "what do you think". Why is he asking this question? For a number of reasons, reason number one, he has been married longer than one day and knows if momma ain't happy, ain't nobody happy. Number two, he knows that regardless of how much he may have liked the garage or the backyard, if his wife doesn't feel safe or she feels it is an unstable neighborhood the garage may actually have to be where he sleeps if the house is purchased. Most important, he knows and cares about what the S in the relationship needs and he wants as a loving partner to provide it for the S. If you really wanted to close the transaction you would be identifying the S, addressing their needs and leaving the rest up to the strong desire that S's have for a safe, secure and stable environment. I have seen many iron fisted D's or showing stopping I's brought to their knees by the unmet needs of an S. I forget now whether I was talking about marriages or agents.

SELLING

Meeting the needs of an S seller is a simple as understanding you are selling THEIR HOME, not a house. One more time for all of you D and I agents out there. It is their safe, secure, stable oasis from the world, not a 3bd, 2bth, views, views, views. As you make that listing presentation being able to identify the S in the room will allow you to speak directly to their fears. Remember they are not concerns, or interest, they are fears. And unless you treat them as fears you will not be able to capture their confidence. They want to know how will you handle the hordes of unknown people who will be traveling through their home. How will you ensure that the horror story they heard from their neighbor about the extended or canceled escrows will not occur? How will you protect them from having to talk to anyone, especially that other agent? And the list goes on and on. The S will overlook the fact that you don't look anything like the picture on your card if they believe that you are going to protect them.

There is not another situation in the real estate industry that resembles a knight in shining armor going forth to slay the dragon, like agents working with S buyers. The best thing you can do for your business when someone comes to you looking for a home is to spend a few minutes asking the necessary questions to determine their personality. If it turns out you are working with a strong S buyer, (and the math suggest more times than not you will be), you need to, in the best word picture you can draw, help them understand how you will protect them. An S already believes that any interruption to their steady, stable routine is not only an invasion of their privacy, but the most terrifying experience they can imagine. If they knew that you would go find the home they want, at the price they want, help arrange the financing, deal with the obnoxious sellers and their evil agent, and that all they would have to do is wait for you until you arrived with good news. They would sign anywhere. Did you say sign a buyers contract? You don't think I am going to do all that work for free do you? Agents who have been unsuccessful in getting buyers to agree to written relationships never communicated to the S how the agent was going to slay the dragon. So use all of your weapons to become a knight in shining armor or just be the person who takes my horse around to the back and park it please.

SIGNING

If you have properly identified and carefully handled the S relationship throughout the transaction, will you receive a commission check? NO. You will not receive *a* commission check, you will receive three commission checks. Studies support you will receive an average of 3 commission checks for each S relationship. Why? Because they are the most loyal people on the planet. Real Estate professionals are the last people in modern business to use this information to their benefit. Think about your own past corporate background, or someone you know. Were they asked to complete some sort of skill set testing, or personality profile during the interview process? You think companies do this to see who is going to be the funny person that they hire out of this group? Or maybe you really believe they want to put you in the best position available in their company based on your personality. Guess what? Along with a number of other things they are looking for, they really want to know how long you are going to stay. Why should they put out money and training to someone who will be gone within the year? The question is not how could a person stay with a company so long, the real question is how did the company find these people who stayed so long? How does the company close the deal on these long-term employees? Give the S what the S wants. Show up at the same time, same place, same job, same everything. And the S loves it.

As a real estate professional you must realize that your S clients are going to need this kind of continuity in the transaction. If you manage to get a strong S client and do not provide these services you will always being talking to someone who is scared out of their mind because they are out of their comfort level. Putting an S against the wall with a long list of new experiences will quickly get you a client who feels cornered. Those really unreasonable clients you have had in the past were probably not dictatorial D's, (because by the numbers there really are not that many of them), they were probably scared spit less S's who are about to come out of the corner with fangs ready. The worst of it is, (after you stop bleeding), is that you will never see them again and they were worth a couple more transactions to you. If you want to close the deal with an S, help them understand they are simply going to wake up one morning in their new house and you will handle all of the details. If that sounds like too much work to you, there is a company still looking for employees.

6

Satisfying The Cautious Personality
(The Science)

"C"s have the potential to drive a wooden man crazy! If you tell them they are too pessimistic they will reply, "I am not pessimistic I am realistic." If you tell them that they worry too much they will reply, "I don't worry, I just get concerned."

"C"s are:
Calculating
Conservative
Cautious
Competent
Compliant

"C"s promote quality in products or services in existing circumstances. They are task-oriented, passive people. As thinkers and analyzers, they work on solving problems. High tech is more important than high touch to them. They respond to form and function rather than feelings, therefore reasoning rather than relationship drives them.

"C"s pursue perfection and sometimes carry correctness to extremes. They prefer to accomplish one thing correctly than to partially complete ten tasks. They follow directions and standards very carefully, and they want to comply with the rules while stressing quality in their work. They have very high standards, and they concentrate on details.

"C" teachers may have the most attractive bulletin boards in the entire school, but when they are complimented, they respond, "But look at the upper left hand border, it is a half an inch off!" These picky people pinpoint problems rather than focus on the potential. They are more aware of burdens than blessings. "D"s would say, "Who cares if it is off a little bit at least it is finished." "I"s would probably want to borrow it for them to use next quarter. And an "S"s would politely say, "I helped put it up, could I help you also?"

"C"s are not easy believers. They need explanations and answers. They often have to analyze the problems before exercising their faith. They work well in controlled environments. They tend to be conservative decision makers, checking all the options and leaving no loose ends. They need precision and predictability.

"C"s are diplomatic with most people, but they can also be critical. Weighing their words for effectiveness, they may inflict vicious verbal jabs to make their point. Correctness is their greatest concern. They constantly check for accuracy. They tend to be quite competent, but they are only cautiously confident. Accepting a fact at face value is very difficult because they feel compelled to dig deeper or probe further. This analyzing can be annoying for others, but in most cases their thoroughness is reassuring. Because they aren't satisfied with surface answers, these calculating people turn over every leaf and read every line. Their inquisitive natures consume them. They need in depth answers.

"C"s tend to become experts in specific areas because they absorb themselves in whatever they do. They criticize freely, no matter if it is their performance or another's. Seldom is anything ever 100% right in their eyes. With an eye for quality, they strive to better themselves and others. Finding a better way of doing things is their cup of tea.

They are critical thinkers. They ask, "Why?" and tell you if something could be done better. At times, precise thinking makes them too picky. They can be thorns in the flesh because they are naturally pessimistic.

As passive individuals, "C"s tend to comply with authority. They are not aggressive when presented with a challenge. Instead, they try to find a way to fix the problem. They don't desire to be in control for control sake, but they demand that things be done correctly and in order. They don't respond well to differences. Complying is easier for them than communicating, and they believe silent surrender is better than open confrontation. However, this often leads them to hold grudges, engraving in granite the memories of past offenses. Forgiving and forgetting are very difficult for them.

Because they question everything, including themselves, these critical, calculating people need to be constantly reassured. They focus on problems rather than solutions, and this challenge demands they work in sheltered, stable conditions. The slightest trouble is magnified in their minds, and dealing with more than one problem at a time can be overwhelming for them. "C"s need constant encouragement because they are pessimistic by nature. Their concern for correctness causes them to worry. They seem to doubt more than most.

Quality Control

"C"s want SOPS, standard operating procedures. They dislike uncertainty and want to know exactly when, why, how, where and what. They are most comfortable when order is valued and confusion is limited. They work best under structured conditions, so consistency is critical. Abrupt alterations threaten them with their biggest emotional challenge: the fear of being incompetent. They think change for no good reason is insane. Others may scurry to test a new possibility, but "C"s drag their feet until convincing facts are presented.

The status quo allows them to refine and improve the system. "quality control" is their personal motto. If they cannot do it right, they don't want to do it at all. They are the perfect fit for the job that requires precision and detail. Because they are never satisfied unless they complete the job right, they are the consumers best friend because they sincerely desire to do the best job they can.

"C"s take great pride in their work. They are their own worst critics, but they appreciate recognition of their craftsmanship. They don't seek personal praise, but they appreciate attention for their finished product. You may criticize them, but don't criticize their work. "I"s are very sensitive to personal criticism, but they may not care if someone criticizes their performance. "C"s are just the opposite. They take personal rebuke lightly, but are deeply offended if people dare criticize their work. They enjoy situations that call attention to their accomplishments. They strive to provide first class products and services, and they prefer opportunities that focus on their products rather than themselves.

In Search Of Excellence

"C"s are not adventurous, but they are inquisitive for quality's sake. Search for new thrills is not nearly as important as seeking new truth. They need the balance provided by those who will compromise, and they need others to help them find the medium between opposing views. Often unwilling to compromise, they tend to offend others. Because of their natural ability to see problems, they should be careful about open criticism. They need to allow opportunities for others to state their positions. They would be wise to hold back at times and allow someone else to find flaws and make the first response so they are not perceived as always negative.

Precise, detail work allows them to be most effective, so they should look for jobs that require them to do what working in a supportive environment will provide. They need opportunities for careful planning. Their clarity and objectivity go hand in hand. Having time to think, evaluate, and make corrections is important. They deplore disorganization and carelessness. They prefer specific job descriptions, and they like to know exactly what their job requires. Without this clarity, confusion reigns and frustration results.

Because of their need for explanation, periodic appraisals should be scheduled. They desire feedback and help along the way, and evaluations of their performance from time to time enhances their work. They must learn to respect people as much as they respect their own accomplishments. Because of their strong task-orientation, they tend to get over involved in projects and forget people, but the value of a person exceeds a completed project.

Developing tolerance for conflict is also a very important lesson for cautious, compliant "C"s. Their passive personalities cause them to withdraw and verbally holdback. They tend to run away in order to avoid trouble.

"C" parents, teachers, mates and employees can be very difficult to live and work with. They tend to be too task oriented and often rub people the wrong way. Relationships are built on agreements, and people respond best to those who share a common bond. These naturally critical people need to learn to be more agreeable instead of judgmental. They can become very lonely people because few friends will endure their need to always be right.

"C"s often focus on correctness and miss the fellowship and feelings of others. Compromise is important to healthy relationships. Some people take offense at the thought of compromise, but it is absolutely necessary in marriage. "C" partners need to be more tolerant and forgiving. Their moodiness can kill love. Constantly pressing for perfection can discourage anyone. They need to learn to be more positive and optimistic.

Children of "C" parents often feel like they can never please their parents. The children may clean their rooms, but their rooms are never quite clean enough to suit the parent.

At work, "C" supervisors can erode good attitudes by never complementing their employees. Constant criticism is demotivating. Try focusing on the good your employees do. It will increase their effectiveness.

"C" employees must remember to not complain too much. It makes fellow employees avoid you. It also makes management think you are not a team player, and therefore, your chances for promotion may be affected.

Conflicts

"C"s are experts, even at conflict. They have perfected their way of finding fault in nearly everything. If there is a flaw in the plan, they will find it. They have the intuitive ability to find the weak spots, but faultfinding is extremely annoying to the dreamers and doers. "D"s inevitably clash with "C"s over implementing an idea. "D"s want to do it immediately, but "C"s want to take more time to research and prepare.

Questions, Questions, Questions

"C"S asks question, after question. It is not that they are not smart. In fact, "C"s tend to be very inquisitive and great learners. They need to guard their constant search for answers and learn how to be happy without understanding everything.

"C"s make great students, if their teachers satisfy their quest for knowledge and understanding. "C"s need to avoid against becoming moody, if their search is not being satisfied. "C"s make the most competent, yet often most challenging to work and live with.

THE REAL ESTATE PERSONALITY PUZZLE

(Applying the Science)

SEEKING

Remember when your kids use to follow you around asking you questions. Why this, why that? How come? Who said? Are we there yet? Be prepared for the same set of questions from your C clients. When you go looking for these clients be sure you have your facts in order and under no circumstance try and blow the hot air you did on the I. If you are going to be successful in attracting C sellers you will be pleased to discover you finally get to use all of those facts, figures, charts and other materials designed by your company to dazzle people. The C seller will love it. One word of caution however, you better be sure the facts are correct because the seller will keep the folder overnight and call you in the morning if there are any corrections. How do you know if you have a C seller? There are some obvious clues. If you go to a listing appointment and the prospective client has a notepad, pencil and calculator. C. If you find yourself explaining the presentation instead of delivering the presentation. C. It is okay. You are the professional, act like one. If you do not get the listing you will be better prepared for the next one thanks to your C experience.

C buyers are actually more difficult and I am not sure I would go looking for them. While the C seller will obsess over the details of the sales transaction, there are only so many stages in the transaction before it is over. It is never over for a C buyer. All the questions that drove you crazy with your children are about to multiply tenfold and this time you will have to provide facts to back it up. Try telling a C buyer, "because I said so." C's will ask everything from the obvious, allowable and necessary questions that you will deal with in every transaction, to the absolutely unrelated pursuit of information just for the curiosity of it. Remember you still need to get paid so don't drive your car off the cliff yet, (or theirs either), help is on the way. The only guaranteed way to make it through a C buyer transaction with no police report being filed is to give the C a project to work on. Am I suggesting that you distract the unsuspecting C by appealing to their undeniable, insatiable desire to get to the bottom of a problem? I am not suggesting it, I am telling you it is the only chance you have. Remember you probably have a worried S waiting in the wings who is the spouse to this C person. The worried S knows it will never be over as long as the C is working on the "find a house problem". Give the C legitimate projects to work on, set up regular reporting times and get that worried S into a house. If that doesn't work, C-ya.

SELLING

Selling a C is like trying to convince your children that broccoli is good for them. As a parent you know that it is, you also know that convincing the child of that will require finding the reason that makes the most sense to the child. But you **will** have to find a reason. Working with a strong C seller will necessitate you staying in the convince mood at all times. But you will have to convince with facts not persuasion. If a C seller wants to know what it is going to cost to sell the house, show them the net sheet. I know that is not something you always want to do at the beginning of a client relationship but here it is necessary. If the C seller wants to know how title works, (here is where the projects start), have them make an appointment with the escrow office and have your trusted officer explain in long detail how the process works, (make sure the C gets the title officers card before you leave, sounds cruel, but it may save your life). If the C seller wants to know something about the contract, (next project), pull out a copy of every contract possibly related to the transaction that you can find, send it home with them. If three days later they have questions about the contract direct them to the related local or state law that produced the contract language and get a report from them in three or four days. You get the idea.

The same is true for the C buyer. If there is some question about the property lines, you will want to encourage them to go to the county recorders office and get copies of the related maps and do the research. I know what you are thinking. You are thinking, "How am I suppose to get my client to go do the work that they want me to be doing?" You just have not caught on yet have you? If the D buyer says I need it, get it, they want to know you can follow orders. If the I buyer says I need it, forget it, because tomorrow you will tell them this is better for you. If the S buyer says I need it, assure them you will take care of it, that is all they really wanted anyway. If the C buyer says I need it, show them where to find it and you keep looking for the house. Am I sure this will work? Call me and I will give you list of over 15,000 names of agents who stopped being controlled by their client base by understanding who they were dealing with and what that personality needed. Here is the last C question you will ever have to answer, what do you have to lose?

SIGNING

How do you get a C seller to sign anything? Make sure they have seen it all before. I know after years as a broker one of the things agents love to do is unleash all this necessary documentation at the close of a transaction. They assume since the seller will not understand it anyway, it just creates problems to expose the clients to the information contained in the paperwork. If you see someone walking out of a scheduled signing before all the documents are signed, it is a C. Shove one piece of paper under the nose of a C seller and watch the hands of time grind to a stop.

C's are not only a major obstacle to the closing because they are going to read everything, here comes the scary part; they are going to ask you to explain it. In your haste to complete the transaction you forgot that the C will want to know the answer, and if you don't know the answer the last thing you will see is you deal walking out the door. If you want to close the deal on a C seller, the final signing contains absolutely no new information, you see?

No new surprise information for the C buyer either. That is why regular reporting times are so important when dealing with a C buyer. If you will train them for new information at regular intervals and provide them with tasks to complete in between reports, then new information is not seen as new information just more information in a long list of more information. And there is nothing that a C loves more than more information. At some point you will have to be brave enough to say, that is all the information. If after a period of time that you feel is sufficient to answer the majority of the C's questions, (remember you will never answer all of their questions), and remembering that your are in business to make a living, you must be able to help the C client to understand it is time to move. You may even want to use the house they are looking to buy as the illustration by saying, "remember that beautiful porcelain throne we saw in the master bath, it is time to either use it or.......................

7

Discovering Your Behavioral Blends
(The Science)

Our personalities are composites of four identifiable temperaments. No blend is better than the other. Each blend simply describes the complexity of our personalities. Only 15% of people have a predominate "D" or "I" or "S" or "C" personality. The other 85% have a mixture of two or three specific types such as:

D/I, S/C, I/S, D/C, I/C, D/S, or I/S/C.

There are actually 256 possible composites, but we will focus on twenty-one behavioral blends. Study the brief paragraph descriptions in this section. You may be a combination of two specific profiles. You can also have some characteristics of other types, but usually, people fit into one or two behavioral blends. Each set of descriptions begins with a brief summary of that single, unblended personality type which is followed by blends of that type.

Dr. John Geier, who developed the original Performax Personal Profile System, originally identified 18 blends which he called "Classical Patterns." His research concluded that these patterns were the most common blends. Since that time, Dr. Geier has added three more patterns which are blends of three types. Please note; There are two D/Is but no D/S. The two are included because there are two distinct varieties of this blend, and the D/S is omitted because these people are described in the S/D blend.

D: Determined Doers

"D"s are dominant and demanding, and they want to win at all cost. They don't care about what people think, they want to get the job done. They are insensitive to others feelings. They are determined to get going, but they need to be more attentive to details. They are motivated by serious challenges to accomplish tasks.

D/I: Driving Influencers

"D/I"s are bottom line people. They are much like dynamic influencers, but Driving Influencers are more determined and less inspirational. They are strong doers and able to encourage others to follow. They need to be more cautious and steady. They often get involved in too many projects, so they need to slow down and focus on one thing at a time. They are motivated by opportunities to accomplish great tasks through a lot of people.

D/I: Dynamic Influencers

"D/I"s are impressive and demanding. They get excited about accomplishing tasks and looking good. Determined and driven, they influence large crowds best. They can be too strong and too concerned about what others think. They can have good communication skills and are interested in people, but they need to be more sensitive and patient with the feelings of others. Slowing down and thinking through the projects are crucial. They are motivated by opportunities to control and impress.

D/C: Driven and Competent

"D/C"s are determined students or defiant critics. They want to be in charge while they collect information to accomplish tasks. They care more about getting a job done and doing it right than being kind and considerate, but they would be more influential if they were more aggressive and careful. Motivated by opportunities to share and shine, they readily induce others to follow them.

S/D: Steady Doers

"S/D"s get the job done. They prefer stable surroundings and are determined to accomplish task. As a quiet leader, they relate best to small groups. They don't like to talk in front of large crowds, but they want to control them. They enjoy secure relationships, but too often try to dominate people. They are motivated by sincere challenges that allow them to accomplish tasks systematically. They make good friends even though they have a driving desire to succeed.

S/C: Steady and competent

"S/C"s are stable and contemplative people. They like to research and discover the facts, and they like to weigh the evidence and proceed slowly to a logical conclusion. They enjoy small groups of people, but they don't like speaking in front of large crowds of people. They are systematic and sensitive to the needs of others, but they can also be critical and caustic. They are loyal friends but can be too fault-finding. They need to work on their enthusiasm and optimism. They are motivated by kindness and by opportunities to accomplish tasks slowly and correctly.

C: Cautious Competent

"C"s are logical and analytical. Their predominant drive is careful, calculating, compliant, and correct behavior. When they feel frustrated, they may withdraw in despair, or in contrast, as they may become hyperactive. They need others to answer their questions patiently. They are not sensitive to the feelings of others, and they can be critical and crabby. They prefer quality and reject phoniness in others. They are motivated by explanations that stimulate their thinking.

C/S: Competent Specialist

"C/S"s have to be right. They like to do one thing at a time and do it right the first time. Their steady and stable approach to things makes them reserved and cautious. They are consistent and careful, but seldom take risk or try new things. They don't like speaking to large crowds but will work hard behind the scenes to help groups stay on track. They are motivated by opportunities to serve others and to do things correctly.

C/I/S: Competent, Influencing Specialist

"C/I/S"s like to do things right, impress others, and stabilize situations. They are not aggressive or pushy people. They enjoy both large and small crowds. They are good with people and do quality work. They are sensitive to do what others think about them and their work. They need to be more determined and dominant. They can do things well, but are slow in decision-making. They are capable of doing great things through people, but they need to be more self-motivated and assertive. They are stimulated by sincere, enthusiastic approval and logical explanations.

C/S/D: Competent, Steady Doers

"C/S/D"s are a combination of cautious, stable, and determined people. They are task-oriented, but they care about people on an individual basis. They don't like to speak in front of crowds. They prefer to get the job done and do it right through small groups instead of large groups. They tend to be serious and are often misunderstood by others as being insensitive. "C/S/D" types really care for people, but they just don't show it openly. They need to be more positive and enthusiastic.

I: Inspirational Influencers

"I"s are impressive people. They are active and excited individuals. Approval is important to them. They can have lots of friends if they don't overwhelm people with their enthusiasm. They can be sensitive and emotional, but they need to be more interested in others and willing to listen. They don't like research unless it makes them look good. They often do things to please crowds because they are entertainers. They need to control their feelings and think more logically. They often outshine others and are motivated by recognition.

I/D: Inspirational Doers

"I/D"s are super sales people. They love large groups. They are impressive and can easily influence people. They need a lot of recognition, and they often exaggerate and talk too much. They jump into things without thinking them through, so they need to be more studious, reflective, and cautious. If they are not careful, they live to please the crowd and get themselves into trouble. They make inspiring and determined leaders.

I/S: Inspirational Specialist

"I/S"s are influential and stable. They love people and people love them. They like to please and serve others, but they don't like time controls or difficult tasks. They want to look good and encourage others, but they often lack organizational skills. They can follow directions and do what they are told, but they should be more concerned about what to do, than with whom to do it. They are motivated by interaction and sincere opportunities to help others. Whether they are up front or behind the scenes, they like to influence and support others. They make good friends and obedient workers.

I/C: Inspirational and Competent

"I/C"s are inspiring yet cautious. They size up situations and comply with rules in order to look good. They are adept at figuring out ways to do things better than a lot of people, but they can be too persuasive and too concerned about winning. They are often impatient and critical, and they need to be more sensitive to individual feelings even though they are very sensitive about what others think about them. They don't like breaking the rules, and they don't enjoy taking risk. They need to try new things and sometimes go against the crowd. They are careful communicators.

S: Steady Specialist

"S"s are stable and shy, and they don't like changes. They enjoy pleasing people and can perform repetitive tasks. Secure, non-threatening surroundings are important to them. They make good friends because they are so forgiving, but other people some time take advantage of them. They need to be stronger and learn how to say no. Talking in front of large crowds is usually difficult for them. They are motivated by opportunities to help others.

S/I: Steady Influencers

"S/I"s are sensitive and inspirational. They have lots of friends because they are tolerant and forgiving. They don't hurt people's feelings and can be very influential, but they need to be more task-oriented. They need to learn to finish their work and do it well. They like to talk and should pay more attention to instructions.

I/D/S: Inspiring, Driving, and Submissive
"I/D/S"s are impressive, demanding, and stable. They are not as cautious and calculating as those with greater "C" tendencies. They are fairly active, but they are sensitive and steady. They seem to be people oriented, but they can be dominant and decisive in their task-orientation. They need to be more contemplative and conservative. Taking charge and working with people are more important to them than details.

D/I/C: Dominant, Inspiring, and Cautious
"D/I/C"s are demanding, impressive, and competent. They tend to be task oriented, but they are comfortable before crowds. They need to increase their sensitivity to others. They don't mind change. Active and outgoing, they are also compliant and cautious. They like to do things correctly, but they also influence others to follow because their verbal skills combine with their determination and competence. Security is not as important to them as looking good.

Straight Mid-Line
A Straight Mid-Line Blend occurs when all four plotting points on the DISC assessment are in the middle area of the graph. This may indicate that the person is trying to please everyone. This person may be experiencing intense frustration as a result of this behavior. When this person takes the profile, he may answer in ways he thinks

others want him to answer instead of his real thoughts and preferences. He can complete another profile several months later to get a more accurate reading.

Above Mid-Line

Some patterns indicate unique struggles an individual may be having. An Above Mid-Line Blend occurs when all four plotting points are above the mid-line. This may indicate the person feels compelled to over-achieve.

Below Mid-Line

A Below Mid-line Blend occurs when all four plotting points are below the mid-line. This may indicate that the person feels insecure and is not really sure how to respo

(THE REAL ESTATE PERSONALITY PUZZLE)

(Applying the Science)

SEEKING

Now that you have a better understanding as to how to deal with the different personalities of your client base, lets spend some time talking about you. Seeking out your personality type and learning how to implement the use of your personality in your business is the most fundamental step you can take in becoming a top producing agent. You should spend as much time as possible reviewing the behavioral blends I have described until you find the one that most closely matches yours. Once you have sought out and feel comfortable with the blend that best suits you it is important to learn how to interact with the other blends. Seeking and choosing the blend that describes you may sound like the most obvious step to take, however, few agents will do it. Why would any agent ignore the most basic of all steps to becoming successful? One word, SEMINARS!

Admit it, you have been to so many seminars and purchased so much seminar stuff from former top producing agents that you have a library of stuff you have never used. I call them CULT CAMPS. They have all the trappings of any cult you have ever read about. There is always this one dynamic person, (I), who appeals to the deep desire in the majority of the people, (S), to become all that the I is and has. Not only does the CL, (cult leader), promise you that all that they have can be yours, they provide you access to that promise through their teachings. The CL provides the faithful with CD, (cult doctrine), on a cd, that is offered for free if other CD is purchased on the set of cd's that have been conveniently packaged for your trip home. Usually the only thing missing at cult camp are autographed pictures of the cult leader, oh, I forgot, you did get their autographed picture on the notebook and workbooks. It is time you learned how to see the CL and their CD in the light of your D, I, S, C. It is not that all the material is not useful, it is that it must be interpreted and applied through your personality to be practical or you will just be adding to you cd collection.

SELLING

Selling your self and your services are only as good as your understanding of yourself and your services. Think about your particular behavioral blend. Do you really think that as a CS you will be able to walk away from a seminar held by an ID and present their material the way they presented it? Do you wonder why it never seems to have the impact on your clients that it had on you? It is because it is being filtered through your personality, your behavioral blend, and if you have no idea what that is, you now know why the client has no idea what you are saying. I have been a broker in the real estate industry in the San Francisco bay area for many years. After my son graduated from college and tried his hand at the corporate world for a while he decided to reconsider a career in real estate. My son who has had access to my training materials and my experience in the industry made a very deliberate decision to not conduct his business the way I conduct my business. Here is what both businesses look like and then you decide which one of us has which personality type and behavioral blend.

Early in his career he would call and say, "my client is having a hard time coming up with the financing". I would say, "you should have looked at his money before your started spending time". His reply, "I looked at his money and knew it was going to be difficult for them, but they really need a house". Do they need a house more than you need to get paid, I would ask? It shouldn't take you too long to figure out the basic personality type differences. Which personality is going to make the most money? The one that knows which personality they have. He knows that he has a strong care giving thread in his personality and to ignore that would make business cold and impersonal to him. So, instead of trying to duplicate some other person's personality and method of selling, he caters to clients that need a little extra attention. He loves it, his clients love it and in the large office he is affiliated with there is no end to agents with my personality who are willing to give him clients because they don't want to spend the time. Who is making the most money and having the most fun? The person who knows the most about who they are and how their personality and behavioral blend factor into a transaction. So stop chanting the guru mantra and say goodbye to CL's with their CD's on their 4-volume set of cd's and learn about yourself.

SIGNING

Closing the deal on who you are and what your behavioral blend is will only come with knowledge and practice. It actually becomes your personal signature. Your signature on every transaction, which begins to separate you from other signatures since no one signature is like another. Then after some time and practice your personal signature on every transaction, (based on you understanding and applying your behavioral blend), is what will distinguish you from other agents. Not the books or tapes or cd's you buy and try to duplicate in your daily routine, but the clear, distinct you that comes out in everything you do. And after you have a clear understanding of your behavioral blend you can understand other blends so that you are meeting the needs of your clients in a way no other agent ever has. I know you have heard the marketing phrase, some will, some won't, so what, next! Sounds like a great way to appease your need to go find new clients. Run through as many people as possible until you can find a deal. It may work as a way to set up appointments but it is no way to stay in business long term. Successful real estate professional are looking for residual business. You want to establish long-term repeat business. The only way to do that is to know yourself and your client.

8

Practical Applications

Each of us needs specific, practical applications to enhance our strengths and avoid our weaknesses. This chapter contains general suggestions to help people of each personality type.

Seeing our behavior in others can help us understand ourselves. By recognizing the quirks of those around us, we can improve our own behavior. Often, the things we hate in others are the very things we struggle with in our own lives.

Practical application is making knowledge work. If we don't know how to use knowledge, it is worthless. Being people smart is knowing why people do what they do. but being personality wise is knowing what to do about it. The tragedy in most relationships is that people don't even have the basic knowledge of human behavior. Understanding how and why we are the way we are is important, but practical application is what makes our knowledge powerful. After all is said and done, we need to apply what we learned. The goal is to apply truth in our specific areas of improvement. Life is a journey toward maturity. We are always improving but never arriving. It is a challenge and an adventure, a steady and reasonable journey.

Did you notice that I used D, I, S, and C terms in the last sentence. "D"s respond to challenges. "I"s love the adventure. "S"s desire steady and stable emphasis, and "C"s look for the reasonable things. We respond to according to our personalities. Practical application helps us recognize our strengths and weaknesses so that we can use our strengths to overcome our weaknesses. Some of the greatest lessons come from on the job training. All the books and seminars in the world can never compare to the lessons we learn from life's experiences.

Experience is a great teacher. The problem is we often fail to learn from our experiences. We have learned that people respond in many different ways. We respond according to our own personalities, but each person we meet with has his or her own personality, and the clash of different temperaments causes conflict. Volumes have been written about human behavior, but wisdom is attained only by using the knowledge we acquire. Experience provides knowledge, but wisdom provides practical application.

Practical Application For "D"s

"D"s must learn how to be team players. Their desire to be in charge tempts them to fly solo. Although they may be able to do some things better by themselves, they can be more influential as a part of a team. They need to train themselves to include others in their decision-making. They also need to be aware of the needs and drives of others. Working with "D"s who refuse to play second fiddle to anyone can be exasperating. Often they don't understand their emotions and actions. They can benefit from a clear explanation of why they have such determination.

"D"s Need Choices Not Commands

"D"s don't like being told what to do, so it is important to give them choices. Instead of telling a "D" child that he must go to bed at 9:00, tell him he can chose between going to bed at 8:30 or 9:00. Ask him, "Which time do you chose?" Explain who is the boss, and teach them responsibility by allowing them to make some decisions for themselves. Make sure they realize that there are consequences if they do not act responsibly. Get "D" children to agree beforehand on the punishment or discipline they will receive if they violate the rules.

Do not let "D"s control you. They need parameters for their behavior and actions. They stretch the limits, so you must let them know how far is too far. They desperately need good role models for self-control. Show them how to stay in control by remaining calm while dealing with them.

"D"s Under Authority

"D"s must learn how to respect authority figures such as the police, teachers, and bosses, even though these people seem to make life difficult. They do not enjoy being submissive. There is something in them that cries for independence and wants freedom, but the worst bondage is enslavement to one's own emotions and actions. True freedom comes through being under authority. We cannot truly possess authority until we learn to submit to authority. The most powerful people in the world are under some type of authority. When we learn to work in healthy dependence on others instead of defiant independence, they will be more successful. "D"s typically see submission as weak or cowardly, but this can be used as a tremendous opportunity to show them what strength under control really means. They lose their authority if they lose the respect of others. Then they have no platform to influence people. Understanding the principle of respect for authority is imperative for them.

Practical Applications For "I"s

"I"s are driven by their strong desire to impress and influence. They want to be recognized for their accomplishments, because rewards are important to them. Speak positively about them in public. Parents would be wise to phone a friend or relative and share how pleased they are about their children's accomplishments. Every child deserves this, but these children thrive on personal recognition. "I"s like to look good. "I"s enjoy excitement – the more enthusiasm the better. "I"s need opportunities to express themselves. Asking them to obey without allowing them to question or share their feelings can be frustrating for them. It is not that they are questioning authority, they simply need to talk when they feel pressure. Given enough time, some "I"s will even talk themselves into doing what they resisted. Don't try to out talk them. Wait patiently and listen until they are ready for your response. That may never happen, so ask them to let you talk when they are finished. They will interrupt you and take off on another long-winded discourse. Again, wait for a while and then remind them you never finished. This may happen several times, but each time you are building a stronger case for them to learn they need to improve their listening skills.

They Talk Too Much

Once they realize how patient you have been, you will have enough time to share your thoughts. They probably won't listen well, but it will make them think. This process helps "I"s understand what you are trying to say.

It is usually a good idea to ask "I"s to share what they think you have just said to them. Do not condemn them for not listening if they get it wrong. Simply question yourself for possibly not making your words clear enough, and then rephrase your statement. Give them another chance to explain what you are saying until you both come to an agreement about the conversation. That is good advice for everyone, but "I"s especially need to learn how to be slow to speak and quick to hear.

"I"s need to learn how to share the limelight. They are usually talented, and they love to show off, but they may have a problem with pride and an intense desire for others to notice them. Help them overcome this tendency by complimenting their ability to handle losing or by explaining how impressed you are when they are willing to play second fiddle. It takes a big person to allow others to receive the credit he may deserve.

Disciplined Feeling

"I"s need to learn how to reflect and study. Those who are students have the potential to make excellent grades, but they sometimes fail because they socialize too much. They don't like to miss any of the action anywhere. Parents can use the "I" child's desire to impress others as a means of encouraging him to obtain better grades. Reward them with the kinds of things that will improve their self-images, like new clothing or a phone of their own. Also, use discipline which motivates them to study, such as no phone privileges until they have finished their studies.

Suggest that they study with a friend, preferably a "C", who will help the "I" be more thorough in his work. Use video or cassette resources to help maintain his attention span. Find creative teaching methods to relieve them from sitting still for long periods. Get them to study in shorter intervals, ten or fifteen minutes at a time, and encourage them to tell you what they have learned. Invite them to communicate it in a song or even a rap. This may test your patience as a parent, but it could be exactly the motivation the child needs to succeed.

Practical Application for "S"s

"S"s respond best to kind, thoughtful people. Avoid raising your voice or losing your temper with them. They need to be in a secure, calm environments to function at their best. They don't respond well to intense or loud behavior. They back away from unstable situations and unsettling challenges. They are not risk takers and are not comfortable around aggressive people. If possible avoid putting them on the spot.

"S"s don't become easily excited. They may sometimes seem to be disinterested or bored, but it is simply their steady nature to appear so. They are likely to become your best friends because of their sense of undying loyalty. They will stand by you and help you in any way they can.

Time To Recover

Give "S"s plenty of time to adjust. They prefer slow and gradual changes and need time to respond without being pushed. They don't like surprises. If you know there is going to be a change, warn them far enough in advance so they can prepare for it. They usually are not resistant people, but they will be less than enthusiastic if they are not given enough space and time to adapt to change.

High touch is important to them, and they want to feel like a part of the family. Greet them by hugging or grasping their hand with both of yours. Everyone needs intimacy, but "S"s respond the best to a warm and sincere touch. People-oriented individuals must learn to guard against being naïve. They tend to be manipulated by others because of their kind and gentle demeanor, and one of the most important things "S"s need to learn is how to say, no. They tend to agree to do everything people ask them to do. They are vulnerable, people take advantage of them.

Assertiveness training is a practical help. As difficult as they may find it, they can learn to stand strong. Their love for people and sense of loyalty make them easy prey for opportunistic, unscrupulous individuals. They need to be cautious and ask questions before they trust others. "S"s should not feel guilty for saying "no" or worry that they may have hurt people or let the group down.

Don't Work Harder

"S"s need to learn how to turn a request for help into an opportunity to challenge others. They can be more assertive and stimulate others to take more responsibility. They can be bold enough to challenge a "D" to volunteer, enthusiastic enough to stimulate an "I" to get involved, and convincing enough to get a "C" to respond. Leadership is the "S"s most difficult task, but they can be excellent leaders if they learn to be assertive. Because they cringe at the thought of pioneering, they should become involved in projects that stretch their comfort zone. Learning how to adapt and respond to new stresses can be helpful. They have the potential to turn into turtles, retreating into their shells to protect themselves from the possible danger of being bruised and bumped. Taking a public speaking course may be the ultimate challenge for them. The thought of getting up in front of people and speaking may be terrifying, but this experience can result in tremendous growth.

Practical Advice for "C"s

The best advice for "C"s is to be willing to settle for less than perfection. Their constant inquiries can be nerve racking; their need for answers causes stress in their relationships. Recognizing their need to fully understand will help others cope with their inquisitiveness. Ask: "Why do you ask, Why?" This question forces them to think through their question and perhaps answer it for themselves.

Know It All's

"C"s are usually not being disrespectful when they ask questions. They just want explanations. Their drive to comprehend causes them to appear rebellious. Actually, they just want to go by the book, but if they don't understand, they can be negative and condemning. Stimulate them to think through situations on their own and allow them to use their initiative to be competent. Reason goes a long way with them, but typically, explanations create more questions for them to ask. Patience is a great virtue in dealing with them. They tend to be more task-oriented than other people. Feelings are not as important to them, so they may say or do things that seem cold and uncaring. Don't try to appeal to their emotions. Appeal to reason. Recognize that they tend to be moody when they are deep in thought. They usually are not mad or upset, they just act like it. Give them some room. They may misunderstand and demonstrate confusion by expressing displeasure.

Stinging Words

These naturally critical people can be very caustic. Under pressure they can shoot straight, however, they avoid conflict whenever possible. When they feel threatened they attack. They say what they think, and they think what they say, so they are often right on target.

This characteristic of telling it like it is often gets them into trouble because most people don't like to hear the truth. They need to learn how to speak the truth in love and season their speech with sensitivity.

"C"s are party poopers. They dump cold water on ideas faster than anyone, but what they have to say is often very insightful. It is important to learn to listen to their advice even though they may be critical and negative. Be careful not to miss their wisdom because you don't like their attitude. Others' responses to their concerns affect their participation. Many sit and stew, contributing nothing because they were criticized for being negative. They need to be more positive. Occasionally they need to search for the pot of gold at the end of the rainbow instead of finding the pitfalls along the way. They should whistle, sing, smile more, and they will see how much better life can be.

They can take this advice and improve the quality of their lives and the lives of those around them who are tired of their gloom and despair. These critical, observant people are usually accurate in their negative appraisals, but most people don't want friends who are always right. They want friends who will forgive and forget. Friends, who pick each other up, not tear each other down.

Developing People Skills

"C"s can develop their social skills by becoming involved in social activities or taking up a hobby that involves others. Finding activities which force them to relate and express their feelings will help them to come more sensitive. Above all, they should avoid their natural tendency toward depression by learning to control their feelings of inadequacy or incompetence. They need to relax and learn how to enjoy life. They don't always have to understand or explain everything. These cautious people tend to be very competent, but they don't care much about friendships. They tend not to be people oriented, but some of them feel very lonely. Perhaps a lack of friends is the result of being too negative and critical of others. "C"s need to develop their people skills. If they do, "C"s can be the best friends anyone has because they will always tell the truth.

9

Handling Conflict

Every personality has hot buttons. Everyone can act like a "D" when pushed too far. The following descriptions are tendencies or personalities when they are under pressure. Often, the greatest hindrances to healthy relationships are personality conflicts. Positive individuals, desiring to build good relationships, are often discouraged because of misunderstandings and clashes with others. The following is designed to help you discover why people do what they do under pressure and why you may conflict with others. Life's success principles on how to handle conflict are clear. The problem is many people are not aware of their sensitive spots. Everyone needs to learn more about avoiding and resolving conflicts. Review the following pages with your particular behavior blend in mind. Read each section to see how you may respond as a specific personality type. Also consider how you may respond differently because of your hot and cold buttons. To improve your effectiveness, control your personality.

Never use them as excuses for poor behavior. Most problems today are not technical, they are relational.

How Specific Personality Types Respond To Conflict

"D"s

Under pressure "D"s become dictatorial, domineering, demanding, angry, intense, forceful, direct and bossy.

Their sources of irritation are weakness, indecisiveness, laziness, and the lack of discipline, planning, purpose, direction, authority, control and challenge.

"D"s need to back off, seek peace, relax, think before reacting, control their responses, and be patient, loving, friendly, loyal, kind and sensitive.

"I"s

Under pressure "I"s become hyper, overly optimistic, immature, emotional, irrational, silly, wordy and selfish.

Their sources of irritation are disinterest, slowness, pessimism, details, time restraints, antagonism, doubt, structure and the lack of enthusiasm and team participation.

"I"s need to listen, count the cost, control their emotions, and be humble, strong, disciplined, punctual, careful with words and conscientious.

"S"s

Under pressure "S"s become subservient, insecure, fearful, weak willed and withdrawn. This person sympathizes too much and may be naïve.

Their sources of irritation are pushiness, instability, inflexibility, anger, disloyalty, insensitivity, pride, discrimination and unfairness.

"S"s need to be strong, courageous, challenging, aggressive, assertive, confrontational, enthusiastic, outgoing, expressive, cautious and bold.

"C"s

Under pressure "C"s become moody, critical, contemplative, negative and worrisome.

Their sources of irritation are incompetence, disorganization, foolishness, dishonesty, inaccuracy, wastefulness, inconsistency, blind faith and false impressions.

"C"s need to loosen up, communicate, and be joyful, positive, tolerant, compromising, open, trusting and enthusiastic.

10

Warnings

One of the universal questions of life is, "why do people do what they do?" The reactions of others – and or ourselves – sometimes surprise and confuse us. The question clamors for an answer, especially among families and business relationships. Why do people who live or work together respond so differently in similar situations?

The answer is simple yet profound. We do what we do because we are prewired a certain way. Every person is wired with an intricate design of personality and drives from the womb to the grave. This design and environmental engineering has made us the way we are. Our motivational pattern should never be an excuse for poor behavior, but it can provide keen insight for understanding why we do what we do.

We want to make it very clear that this study of human behavior explains normal, human actions and reactions. Other disciplines recognize abnormal behaviors.

Psychologists and psychiatrists have looked at abnormal behavior for decades. We are not going to deal with the short circuits in brain synapses, chemical imbalances, and psychiatric disorders which cause people to do some crazy things. We are focusing on the normal everyday problems people have with their feelings, thoughts, and actions.

We don't want anyone to look at the explanations in this book as an excuse for irresponsibility. People in our society spend a lot of time trying to find an excuse for their actions. Everyday we hear of someone who blames his past, parents, peers, or pressures for their wrongdoing. There are legitimate cases of abuse and abandonment in which people have reason to blame others, but most of us have overcome our problems and are now responsible adults.

FEELINGS

One of our greatest concerns deals with feelings. How we respond to our feelings can make or break us. Feelings, in and of themselves, are neither good or bad. They are just neutral and natural responses to our environment, but the world is full of people who can't cope with their feelings. They use their feelings as excuses for irresponsible behavior.

Feelings are the mechanisms that grab our attention. Emotions are the funny bones that tell us that something just happened. Sometimes we laugh, sometimes we cry, but we definitely respond in some way. We need to learn where these feeling come from in order to control our behavior. What we mean by where these feelings come from is the scientific understanding of our basic human behavior, our natural responses to the pressures of life.

We are not suggesting that all of us need to conduct a deep and difficult exploration into our past that sometimes becomes an excuse for poor behavior. Though we accept the fact that some people suffer today because of their past, many more people use their past as an excuse for irresponsible behavior. Wounds of the past need to be grieved, and the offenses forgiven so we can move on to maturity. That can be a painful process, but it is necessary if we want to be whole, responsible, loving people. Responsibility is what makes us behave in a rational way rather than an irrational way.

Excuse abuse today has become a national epidemic. Like the common cold everyone seems to be catching it. We all have problems, disappointments and struggles in life. We can deal with them in a normal, responsible way or we can choose fight or flight in reaction to our unresolved hurt and anger.

PSYCHIC SCAM

A serious problem often arises when we begin to study human behavior. Sometimes people equate reading people to psychic ability. Some think personality profiling is psychic or like mind readers. The study of human behavior is not psychic. It is simply the understanding of why people do what they do from a normal perspective. We agree we have to be especially careful about those who use so called science about either one. Astrologers and psychics really concern us. There is nothing scientific about either one. Astrology is a good example of how some people try to explain our behavioral types by the alignment of the stars in the galaxies. Issac Newton, one of the greatest scientists who ever lived, wrote "Celestial Mechanics" in 1666, in which he disproved astrology. To think the stars can foretell our future when they are controlled by scientific laws set in the heavens is absurd.

We believe psychic predictions are simply random guesses or coincidental happenings. Most psychics are like good gypsies. They learn how to read body language and find little hints along the way. The Public Broadcasting System aired a program in which leading Russian psychics were suppose to be able to describe people from just looking at their photos. The host of the program showed these "world-renowned" psychics the photo of serial killer, Ted Bundy, without their knowledge of his identity. The psychics never mentioned that he was a serial killer, nor that he had been dead for several years. They said that he was alive, doing well and was a very positive person.

When confronted about the truth about Bundy, the psychics complained that the host did not give them enough information. The host was very careful not to influence the psychics who take information and go on fishing expeditions until they find elements of truth. Like good investigators, they know how to uncover the truth, but unfortunately they always give credit to their so-called psychic powers rather than their intuition and investigative skills.

Gypsy Games

Gypsies are perhaps the most skilled at reading people. They live off gullible people who believe a person's palm or Tarot cards can foretell the future. Gypsies are some of the best co artist and human behavior specialist. They know how to read our eyes, facial expressions and body language. Gamblers are also experts at reading people. They know "when to fold them and when to hold them" by reading nonverbal communication.

Around the turn of the century there was a horse in England that was presented to the scientific community as the fist animal that could add and subtract without any human assistance. It was not a trick, and no one helped the horse. It was eventually discovered that the horse had tremendous perception and could detect the slightest hint of approval or disapproval. The horse would tap its hoof on the ground and stop at the correct number when it sensed the approval of people around it. The horse never failed. Then one day, a young girl gave the horse a simple addition problem and the horse failed to answer correctly. Everyone was astonished, then they discovered the girl did not know the answer either! The horse was looking to her for approval, but she couldn't give it. Her slightest hint, a gleam in her eyes, or some little expression when have told the horse when to stop tapping, but the girl was clueless.....and the horse failed. Before that day, some said this horse was psychic, but now you know the truth. So it is with those who claim to foretell the future or have psychic abilities. There is more fraud and blind faith involved than most people want to admit.

Resources For Solving The Personality Puzzle

These instruments are self-administering, self-scoring, and self-interpreting. When you use these profiles, they include everything you need for scoring and interpretation, so there is no waiting and nothing to mail in. You can identify and understand personality types in the convenience of your home, classroom, or office. These profiles are designed to accomplish specific goals, and therefore, are available in a variety of forms.

FOR BROKERS ONLY

I FEEL YOUR PAIN. As a broker I know the headaches, heartaches and heavy lifting that comes from running your own business. And as if the management and administrative responsibilities were not enough to deal with on a daily basis there is this additional problem...........the people. I am not talking about your clients; I am talking about the professional daycare center you are running with all those agents in your office. Your business depends on their productivity but you spend more time putting them in time out then you do seeing the money from their transactions. You ask yourself why did I agree to either have so many agents or to allow that particular agent in my office.

And if being the den mother to a pack of independent minded, non team oriented individuals was not enough, the only way for you to increase market share is to go out and recruit more little rascals just like the ones you already can't control. You are sitting at your desk interviewing what you hope will become a top producer in your office, knowing the entire time that if they are good, they are going to be a problem and if they are no good, they are going to be a problem. Now you know why Brokers are usually the only person in a real estate office who actually has an office, so they can shut the door and pretend the kids are not there.

Just when you think you have all of your children following the rules and starting to behave, another Broker from another office comes along and offers several of your children a bigger lollipop. I know because I am the keeper of lollipops. As the Director of Operations for the largest real estate recruiting firm in the state of California I am aware and a part of all the agent swapping that goes on out there. Don't hate me because it is not me, YOU are the reason it is so easy to kidnap your children. Look at the industry right now. Every franchise is in an all out war to capture as many agents as possible. One franchise comes up with 100% commission structure, and then another comes up with 110% commission structure. If you are keeping track of what is happening in the marketplace you know that there is actually a franchise that offers huge commissions splits along with residual income if you bring other agents into the office. The two fastest growing franchises in America right now offer residuals, retirement, profit sharing, survivor benefits and more. And they will continue to be the fastest growing until the next bigger lollipop comes along. Even before I could finish this book there is a rumble in the industry about a new franchise beginning in a small southern state that has an infrastructure that will allow you to recruit agents throughout the United States and get paid on what these agents are producing. WHEN AND WHERE IS IT EVER GOING TO STOP!

It stops right now, right here. I am going to tell you why we are the largest recruiting firm in the state of California. The Real Estate Personality Puzzle. Why am I not afraid to tell you our secrets? Because I know that the majority of broker/owners are D,s. And as a D you are not wired to take new information and apply it unless you can convince yourself you actually came up with the idea. So you are more inclined to dismiss what I am about to tell you because you can't believe that someone else would have a better idea than you on the subject of recruiting. Well, for over 14 years we have been visiting offices just like yours with our bag of lollipops and delivering them to each agent based on their *personality*. If you office sounds quiet like the kids have gone out to play, they haven't gone out to play, the lollipop man has been in your office and they are just gone.

How would you like to attract the right agents, know what they were going to produce before you hired them, know what problems they might present to the rhythm of your office and be able to keep them as long as you want? Not only keep them as long as you want, but because you understand based on the information I am going to give you, exactly what they need, you could actually show them the door when they don't fit into the scheme of things anymore and actually make them believe it was their idea. How would like to go to sleep at night knowing that your business was no longer being held hostage by the prim Dona agents, the whining agents, the non-producers and the constant threat of the lollipop man? Here is the missing piece of the Real Estate Personality Puzzle.

As I explain for you how to achieve all of the goals I have described so far, I will use the formula that was used during the main section of the book. SEEKING, SELLING and SIGNING. These are the core concepts of the industry and they apply to your search for a manageable and secure business model. I will describe in detail how to seek, sell and sign each one of the four personality types so that your office is finally balanced, manageable, productive and safe from predator brokers.

SEEKING THE D AGENT

You should already know what this agent looks like because, YOU ARE ONE! I know, I know, you are a broker not an agent, but the same personality traits and behavioral blends that put you in the position you are in, are the same traits you are seeking in the D agent. Think about what you have done. You have amassed a vast knowledge of the industry, no one told you what to do, you just went out and did it. No one gave you business, you made business for yourself. You decided early in your career that the best way to control you business was to, **control your business**. You have hammered out relationships with lenders, title companies, service providers, anyone that could streamline and make your business more profitable. You do not leave any part of the transaction up to someone else or to chance. That is what you are looking for in Agent D.

Now be careful. The quickest way to start the next war is to put you (D), in a room with another you (D). This is where learning how to recognize a D and seek a D, because you know first hand what a D can do, has to be tempered with your ability to tone your D down to find the D. I know toning down is not your style; you have done very well for yourself by living large D style, but remember the point of any business is the bottom line. If your D or your Ego, (E does seem to follow naturally after D), stands in the way of your ability to seek Agent D you are losing money! If you want an agent that will increase your market share and not increase your workload, seek a D and control your D all the way to the bank.

SELLING THE D AGENT

Selling a D (who doesn't really want to work for anyone), on the proposition that they need to work for you, requires you to put your E (ego) in neutral, your D (personality) in hiding so that you can really C their personality. Again, think about what you were looking for when you started your career. Control and freedom. This D wants the same. It is important for you to find a way to create at least the appearance of those two opportunities. It is important because you realize that if the D agent really follows their personality path, one day they will no longer be working for you but for themselves. So it is important as they climb their way to the top you are along for the ride.

It is not about manipulation, it is about being able to read the handwriting on the wall. They will bring you the most money, the quickest and with less managerial responsibilities than the other personalities. All you need to do is promise an incremental increase that provides the D agent with more freedom and control and you can hold on to them for as long as possible. One of the ways you can do this, (we have an expanded training manual if you want to know all the ways), you can do this by starting them out in a cubicle with everyone else and then promising them an office of their own as soon as certain production numbers are met. This may sound obvious to you but the mistake brokers make is that they offer this to everyone and wonder why some succeed and some don't. You could offer this to an S all day long and they will never move. Bad news is you actually pushed the S out the door because they cannot meet D production numbers in a D opportunity, but they can reach S productions numbers, the magic is they are the same numbers if you will simply identify and manage the right personality with the right opportunity.

SIGNING THE D AGENT

So you have properly identified the D agent and have piqued their interest with your D offer and opportunity, how do you get them to sign?

Tell them your are talking to two other agents right now for the one position that is available. I did not ask you to exzaturate, just find some way to communicate to this D agent that there is competion for this position. Tell a D there is only limited space available and sit back and watch the selling begin. Instead of you trying to sell them on working for you all of a sudden there is a full out frontal offensive by the D agent to convince you that you can stop searching because they are the one. All this is done not in an effort to control or manipulate. This knowledge can and has been used to that end and that is why many owners of business have decided not to employ the process. They can't control their own D! But if you realize that it is in the best interest of your company to provide the best situation for your staff, so that they can provide the best service to your clients, so that the best interest of your company is achieved then why not do what is best for everyone? And the best for everyone involved is to set the stage for competion between several D's, step back, take the winner and then progressively and incrementally increase the D's opportunities and responsibilities so they can measure their winnings. As the Broker and Owner of the business and as a D yourself, when do you know it is time for the competing D to go? Watch the sales board. For a D who lives and dies by the winnings, if the winnings start to drop off it is probably not a slump. It is probably someone trying to sneak out the back door, in which case you could quietly let them fade into the sunset, or, you could start visibly and publicly interviewing potential new D agents and watch your disappearing D re-create themselves.

SEEKING THE I AGENT

Why would you as a Broker want an I agent? Because they know everybody!! If you remember the description of an I personality you will remember these people are performers. In school they were the class clowns, in college they were the pranksters, comedians and drama majors of the campus. In the workplace they are the loudest, flashiest, most memorable characters at the office. While crowd control sometimes turns out to be one of your primary responsibilities as a Broker if you have a lot of I agents, it is a good problem to have because these guys love and attract crowds. The I agents will do things for your business that no other agent even wants to do. Things like advertising. If you wanted to spend the smallest amount of money possible on getting your companies name out to the public, agree to subsidise in some small way the name and face of any agent who wants to participate in the program. Guess who will jump at any opportunity to see their name and face somewhere, anywhere. With the right number of I agents you could blanket your market area with advertising paid for by performers. Remember I said they know everybody. They know everybody because I's are always looking for an audience to perform in front of. Seeking the I agent is a simple as looking around you to find the loudest, most flamboyant, charming performer in your circle of peers, giving them top billing and watch them perform.

SELLING THE I AGENT

I agents don't need control or money, they need airtime. Some of the top producing I agents in the country were recently interviewed and asked what their GCI last year was, only 36% knew the answer off of the top of their head. The same top producing I agents were asked how many awards had they won the previous year and 100% of them could list in order of market interest the name and reason for the award. That is how you sell an I agent on the idea of coming to work for your company. Offering any personality type something that you or someone else considers valuable is a complete waste of time and money. I have seen so many Brokers either pursue or develop an I agent only to lose them with the promise of what the D Broker always wanted. Control, more money, ownership, I agents believe, because this is who they are and how they live, that if they live loud enough all of those other things will follow. It is not that they are not interested in those things, it is that they want to be recognized along the way of getting those thing or the journey was of no value to them.

If you are going to convince the I agent to come to your company, and believe me the I's have it when it comes to bringing in the business, become their personal talent agent. Help them understand that it is your goal in life to have every man, woman and child in America uttering their name.

SIGNING THE I AGENT

So you have properly identified the I agent and have piqued their interest with the I offer and opportunity, how do you get them to sign?

Tell them that the weekly radio or TV ads are about to run and you were hoping they would accept your offer in time to appear in these new ads. I know, I know, you are saying that is an insidious, manipulative and controlling move to make, (remember first of all you are a D and you can't help it), second of all, the I knows what you are doing and can't wait to sign. One of the many great benefits of understanding personalities is that properly interpreted and purposefully administered, everyone gets what they really want and what is really best for them. Remember to try and curb your own dreams and ambitions in your professional life to facilitate the dreams and ambitions of those you are asking to join your company. Signing the I agent is as simple as making sure your provide them a clear path to their star on the sidewalk. As their broker your are not so much their real estate career manager as you are their talent agent. I's don't want to succeed at real estate, they want to be seen. These are not things that all agents want because not all agents are I's. You could tell an S you were going to bring them up in front of the entire office at the next sales meeting to recognize their achievements and I can guarantee you the S will come up with some mystery illness that prevents them from attending. Your responsibility as a Broker/Owner is to build your business not produce clones. I know they are loud and I know that they are time consuming, but dollar for dollar no one will provide you more exposure and action than an I.

SEEKING THE S AGENT

You will actually have to seek out the S agent. They are the steady, stable backroom producers that rarely come to the spotlight. This agent will become the backbone of your business. You can only have so many D agents before someone is going to be asked to leave, (you can't have more than 3 of you D's running around loose in an office, that is counting you as the broker as one already). And while I's are great for exposure you only have so much time to give to headliners. The S is the agent you want to actively seek to secure a long-term residual business. Seeking an S agent requires constant vigilance and aggressive action, (easy for a D broker). This is true because you will not find an S agent by looking for their ad on the side of a bus, or on a shopping cart at the grocery store. They won't show up at the awards banquets, the marketing meeting or the latest "hoorah we are all going to be rich real estate seminar." How are you going to find the S agents that will become the most predictable and stable part of your companies business? Seeking the S agent is about knowing where to look and most importantly what to offer. I have said it before, let me say it again, "don't offer what _**you**_ want to have, offer what an S wants.

SELLING THE S AGENT

Selling the S agent is not so much a sales job as it is a counseling job. An S wants to know what will it be like here in my new home. A D agent will make into the home they want, an I agent will make sure they know everybody in their new home, but the S agent wants specific detail on what it is going to be like in their new surroundings. They want to feel safe and secure. You might say that real estate is the wrong field for people who want to feel safe and secure, but an S doesn't mind the insecurity of the transaction, they fear the insecurity of their surroundings. A competent S agent knows that they can successfully close multiple transactions, but not unless they are comfortable with where they are working.

Pointing out to these agents the agents in your company that have been there the longest is of great comfort to them. It says you are willing to create an envirnment where they can stay. If you show a D agent all of your old timers, the D agent will just think the old timers are unmotivated, if you show the I agents the old timers they will immediately start jockeying for position to become the more recognized in the office. S agents want to know that you know how to create stability and security. As the Broker, Owner, Manager or full time recruiter for your office you are selling a lifestyle to these consistent producers. Your most effective selling tool for an S agent is to LISTEN to what they need.

SIGNING THE S AGENT

So you have properly identified the S agent and piqued their interest with the S opportunity and offer, how do you get them to sign?

Give them an employment contract and let them chose where they will park, where their desk will be and how long they want to commit to you. STABILITY and SECURITY! You are wondering if you can offer all of this to one agent? Don't worry about it! Guess where an S agent wants to park? In the back so no one can see them. Guess where they want their desk? In the back so no one can see them. Guess how long they want to work for you? Forever! That is why it is so important to properly identify and offer the right personality the right offer. This is not going to conflict with the D agent because you know they want the opposite of the S agent and the D is not going to be there long enough to make it a problem. It is not going to conflict with the I agent because the I agent will want all of the upfront possibilities they can position themselves for, and when they get to pushy you can remind them when they consistently close as many transactions as the S agent they can have what they are asking for. Seeking the S agent is as simple as tracking from the MLS the consistent producers over the last 3 years and asking title companies what agents always show up for the trainings they offer, (D's don't go because they think they are smarter than everyone else, and I's don't go because they can't sit still that long). Selling an S agent is as simple as listening and letting them know that you are aware of their security needs. Signing an S agent is as simple as making someone feel at home.

SEEKING THE C AGENT

Ten years ago it was easy to spot a C agent coming down the street. They had pocket protectors for their pens, not just black pens, pens with different colors for different task. They all had briefcases, not just briefcases with their lunch in them, but briefcases with rulers and tape measurers, cameras, duplicate copies of their files, albums with every business card they had ever collected, cell phones the size of a shoebox and a color coded list of emergency numbers for themselves and their clients. It was easy to spot them and you knew exactly what you were getting when you hired them. An agent who would always be on time, their paperwork would be complete and they were not making promises they could not keep, (nothing personal I agents).

There was a problem though, these agents are so prepared and meticulous that they don't have much patience for the chaos they see around them. They are careful, calculating and often times caustic. But Brokers were still pretty safe because you could recognize them and only hire as many as you could tolerate. In the high tech age they are a little more difficult to identify and if you are going to seek them here is a short list of what you are looking for. In fact it would be in your best interest to provide potential candadites with a list of items you would like to know if they currently or have ever had in their possession. Don't worry about this process being to formal because a D agent will refuse to do it, an I agent will lose the list and an S agent will ask you how to answer the questions, the C agent will be happy take a list, answer the questions and add more just to make sure it is complete. Here is the list, laptop, ipod, blackberry, ditigal camera, GPS, combination cellphone, camera, PDA, digital handheld recorder, leather carrying case for all of the above items, secret decoder ring and a multicolor pen with a computer camera imbedded for virtual realtime tours. If they answer yes to more than five of these items you have found yourself a C agent.

SELLING THE C AGENT

You must have either cutting edge technology or the promise of the technology coming soon. You might even involve them in the origination of the tech program in your office. They want to know that there is some order, heiarchy and cautiousness about your company. This is not the same thing as security for the S agent, it is not security it is order. These are deliberate people who want to plan the work and work the plan. In order to sell them on the opportunity to work in your office they will need to know not only are all the latest tools available but that there is a system in place to implement those tools. It will be your responsibility to convince of these opportunities but you will need to remember there is a cost to selling the C agent. If every word that comes out of you mouth does not come true when they come to your office, (remember they secretly taped the conversation with their concealed digital recorder), they will make your life miserable. You will be confronted everyday about every little detail in your office. A D agent will not bother you will details because they will just make it happen the way they want it to happen, an I agent never even heard the details as they were out the door to entertain the world, the S agent will carefully listen but fully expect someone else to actually take the initiative to attend to the details. If you sell them, PUT IT IN WRITING!

SIGNING THE C AGENT

So you have properly identified the C agent and piqued their interest with the **C** opportunity and offer, how do you get them to sign? PUT IT IN WRITING! You say obviously I will put it in writing, I have all my contracts in writing. I mean, PUT IT ***ALL*** IN WRITING!!!! Every little detail, and this is not just for your protection it is primarerly to help them make the decision to join you firm. When these careful, calculating, capable agents see it all in order in writing, (which is the way they see their entire world), they can make a careful and calculating decision. It does also provide some protection for you in terms of the daily rhythm of your office. When the C agent hits your door with some seemily minor and

Raymond W. E. Beaty

meticulous complaint you best defense and their best opportunity to move on is for you to say, see item # 4 in paragraph B under the subtitle of office responsibilities.

It may sound like these agents are not even worth going after to augment your sales staff. But I am about to tell you something as a Broker that you might not want your agents to know. The majority of college quarterbacks that get drafted into the NFL never play quarterback! They are drafted as quarterbacks, hold up the number on draft day as a quarterback, they are even introduced to all the adoring fans as the future of the team as the new quarterback but it never happens. Do the math there are hundreds of major college programs that turn out incredible quarterbacks but there are less than 30 pro teams. Where do all these guys go, are you ready? They are turned into wide receivers and defensive backs. Why? Because there can only be so many top producers but they still know the game. Are you with me yet? C agents will never be your top producers, they may even be more trouble than they are worth for the rhythm of your office. But they know the game better than anyone. They know the rules, the forms, the contracts, the laws. Careful, calculating, cautious agents make GREAT escrow coordinators! I know how much time you spend cleaning up files and putting out fires that D and I agents create with their poor admin skills. Why not draft a C agent, hold up their number as C agent, introduce them to the office as the C agent and them put them were they will do the most good for the team. They will be happy, you will be happy and the team will be happy.